JOHN ACORN

A
Winter
Birding Guide
for the
Edmonton
Region

Compiled by:

Harry Stelfox *and* Chris Fisher

EDMONTON NATURAL HISTORY CLUB

Copyright © 1998 by
Edmonton Natural History Club

The Publisher:

Edmonton Natural History Club
Box 1582
Edmonton, Alberta
T5J 2N9

Canadian Cataloguing in Publication Data

Main entry under title:

A Winter Birding Guide for the Edmonton Region

Includes bibliographical references and index.
ISBN 0-9684361-0-2

1. Birds—Alberta—Edmonton Region—Identification.
2. Bird watching—Alberta—Edmonton Region—Guidebooks.
3. Edmonton Region (Alta.)—Guidebooks.
I. Stelfox, Harry A., 1948- II. Fisher, Chris C. (Christopher Charles), 1970- III. Edmonton Natural History Club.
QL685.5.A86W56 1998   598'.097123'34   C98-911078-8

Editor: R. Edrea Daniel

Design and Layout: Broken Arrow Solutions ~ Judy Cook

Front Cover Photograph: *Pine grosbeak* ~ Wayne Lynch

Back Cover Photographs: *Young woman with camera* ~ John Acorn
Snowy owl ~ Gordon Court

Cartography: Trevor Wiens

Printing: Alpine Press Ltd., Edmonton, Alberta

PRINTED IN CANADA

HARRY STELFOX

By the time the first snows fall, most of our nesting birds have headed south for the winter. The last remaining flocks of Canada geese are overhead, winging their way to a more hospitable climate, honking as they go. But even as life seems to be on the wane, an awakening is occurring. Winter is the time of year when "winter finches" and other birds that are rare or absent in the summer appear in our city and surrounding communities. Redpolls, pine siskins, grosbeaks and crossbills all arrive, sometimes in large numbers, sometimes small, depending on the food supply. When the bigger flocks do appear in the Edmonton region, the results can be quite dramatic, and not just on your birdseed bill. Seeing hundreds or thousands of waxwings scatter as a merlin tears through the middle of the flock is a sight one does not soon forget.

During the winter, people fill their bird feeders hoping to attract overwintering birds. Well-stocked feeders and appropriately planted backyards may attract a dozen or more species of birds and hundreds of individuals (as well as the occasional mammal). Even when the temperature is hovering around -30° C and the wind is howling, black-capped chickadees will still visit your feeder, for both shelter and food. These dynamic balls of feathers are ever-present in the Edmonton region and are quite fearless, some being so brazen as to take sunflower seeds or peanuts from your hand! It is these qualities that make this bird a perennial winter favourite, even among experienced birders.

Every year, on a crisp winter morning close to Christmas Day, I get up before dawn and meet my crew of keen counters for the Christmas Bird Count. As a rule, the first bird of the day is a chickadee, and by the end of the day our group has generally seen over 20 species. The city of Edmonton count now regularly reports over 50 species each year. Edmonton is the Christmas Bird Count capital of the world, based on the number of people who participate—523 in 1997, most of them casual birders. The count is a great way to start your birding career because beginners are teamed up with someone more expert, and there is a limited number of species you need to identify.

So for those of you who are just getting interested in birds and want to know how to better enjoy them in the winter months, read on. This book will provide you with all the information you need to find and identify the more common winter birds in the Edmonton area. It will give you an idea of how to attract birds to your backyard, and how to prepare and dress for an outside birding adventure. It will also tell you how to get involved in the ever-popular Edmonton area Christmas Bird Counts. Most importantly, this book will help open your eyes to the beauty that surrounds us, even on the bleakest midwinter day.

TERRY THORMIN
Terry first developed an interest in birds in his early teens while living in Montreal. When he moved to Alberta in 1972, it was to take a job with a private ecological consulting firm doing field work on birds in both Alberta and the Arctic. Since then he has taught many courses on bird identification and led many field trips and tours, going as far afield as Ecuador. He presently works for the Provincial Museum of Alberta, where he runs the live Bug Room.

CORPORATE SPONSORS

The production of this guide would not have been possible without the generous financial support of our corporate sponsors, as shown below.

Alberta Sport, Recreation, Parks and Wildlife Foundation: supporting the development of parks; recreation programs and services; and the management, conservation and preservation of fish and wildlife.

Canada Trust—Friends of the Environment Foundation: bringing people together in ways that contribute to the overall health of the Canadian environment.

EPCOR: "We will know we are there when our customers tell us, when our competitors model us and our people, through their behaviour and words, remind us."

Don Lowry, *President and Chief Executive Officer*

Inland Group: actively involved in the protection and preservation of lands and wildlife for future generations.

Interprovincial Pipe Line Inc.— Community-Based Environmental Initiative Program: helping local groups in their commitment to environmental protection, conservation and public awareness.

CONTENTS

TABLE OF CONTENTS...CONT'D

First and foremost, this book is the product of a generous team effort by several members of the Edmonton Natural History Club (ENHC) and the Edmonton Bird Club over a period of a year and a half. More than 15 club members volunteered many hours of their time to develop the book's concept, prepare the text and acquire photographs.

Christie Dean and Melanie Ostopowich, ENHC summer student employees in 1997, helped to flesh out a detailed outline of content for the book and a strategy for its preparation.

Our authors include Marke Ambard, Nicole Anderson, Gordon Court, Christie Dean, Michael den Otter, Dave Ealey, Chris Fisher, Debbie Galama, Alan Hingston, Geoff Holroyd, Jason O'Donnell, Melanie Ostopowich, Christine Rice, Ellen Scott, Harry Stelfox, Lisa Takats and Terry Thormin. A short biographical sketch of each contributor accompanies their section of the text.

Thanks go to John Acorn, Dave Ealey and Chris Fisher for reviewing the accuracy of the species accounts, to Jack Clements for allowing us to draw on his experience with birds, and Dave Ealey for his assistance to the editor.

Several very fine photographs illustrate this guide; their use has been donated by John Acorn, Gordon Court, Ray Cromie, Chris Fisher, John Janzen Nature Centre, Edgar T. Jones, Wayne Lynch, Harry Stelfox and Dena Stockburger. Special thanks go to John Acorn and Gordon Court, who coordinated the photo acquisition and spent many hours in the field last winter photographing specific birds in an appropriate winter setting.

The City of Edmonton Archives provided access to the 1899 photo of Emily Murphy with her well-feathered hat, as well as the hat and feather illustration from Eaton's 1910-11 *Fall and Winter Catalogue*. Yardley Jones kindly provided permission to use his cartoon artwork of the publicity mascot for the 1987 Edmonton Christmas Bird Count.

This project could not have been completed through volunteer efforts alone. Both the Edmonton Natural History Club and Edmonton Bird Club provided significant seed funding to get the project off the ground. Our corporate sponsors, identified on page iv, provided the majority of the finances required to complete the work. Their support enabled us to acquire the professional services of our editor (Edrea Daniel), graphic designer (Broken Arrow Solutions ~ Judy Cook), and printer (Alpine Press Ltd.). We would like to acknowledge the high quality of these services, including a willingness to go the extra mile to ensure a final product that we all can be proud of.

A final thanks go to our feathered companions of the winter season who are the real inspiration for this book and the stimulation for our desire to share with others the joy they bring.

Birdwatching can be an absorbing activity in any season

JOHN ACORN

CHAPTER ONE

BIRDWATCHING IN A WINTER WONDERLAND

Harry Stelfox

Gray jay

WAYNE LYNCH

This book is for anyone in the Edmonton region who wants to maintain contact with the natural world and enjoy its feathered wonders during the winter months.

For our purposes, the winter season usually starts in late October or early November, when colder temperatures and the occasional snow flurry have pushed most migratory birds further south, and it ends in late March or early April, when spring migrants are returning. However, the southern exodus of most bird species during the fall should not cause nature enthusiasts to despair. Many species, such as the black-capped chickadee and blue jay, are year-round residents, whereas others, such as the Bohemian waxwing, snowy owl and common raven, visit us mainly during the winter months. Winter birdwatching is a great way to enjoy nature during this season, whether it is through the kitchen window, during a walk in a neighbourhood park, while driving to work, or as part of a day trip to the countryside for some cross-country skiing.

And no one should feel left out— birding, even in the coldest months, is accessible to virtually all ages and abilities. For example, backyard bird feeding brings untold hours of pleasure to seniors, youngsters and others who may be inclined to stay close to home and mostly indoors during this season. For those who want to get outdoors as well, successful and enjoyable winter birdwatching requires just a bit of organization and planning for the unique conditions of this time of year. This book is your guide to winter birdwatching in the Edmonton region—no matter what form it takes.

For beginner birdwatchers, the great thing about the winter season is that there are only a couple of dozen common species to know. You don't have to face the confusion that can result from having over 300 different bird species around during the spring, summer and fall period. That isn't to say you won't be challenged to identify some less common and intriguing bird species that crosses your path (see Chapter 2).

Another advantage to winter birding is that good habitat conditions are more localized, making it easier to predict where you are likely to see certain types of birds. In fact, having a well-landscaped backyard, supplemented with different types of birdseed, suet and water, is an especially good way to ensure winter birdwatching opportunities and enjoyment. Chapter 3 provides useful ideas on how to attract birds for viewing at home during winter.

Birdwatchers at the University Farm, Edmonton

There are also excellent birding possibilities beyond the backyard. Trips outdoors offer the chance to see several species that are not likely to appear at your backyard feeder. Also, if you go in a group, you will have a chance to share your interests with like-minded folks. Chapter 4 describes winter viewing field techniques that allow you to stay comfortable and have quality birdwatching experiences, even when it is cold and snowy.

Knowing where to look and what birds to expect to see in certain places, enhances your viewing success. Chapter 5 describes key habitats and locations that will improve your ability to observe certain birds.

Chapter 6 provides photos and entertaining descriptions of 32 of the most interesting and common birds you are likely to see during the Edmonton area winter.

Birdwatching can be a solitary pursuit, a family event or a group activity,

depending on your inclination, although many people like to join others to share their experiences. There is no better way to enjoy this camaraderie than through participation in the Christmas Bird Count, an annual event usually organized by a local natural history club or bird club. Chapter 7 describes the Christmas Bird Count phenomenon, its history and conservation value, and how you can get involved.

This book will help you to expand your enjoyment of birds and their surroundings so that you can appreciate them throughout the entire year. And, let's admit it—we don't look just at the birds when we're scanning the backyard or are out on a birding expedition. We enjoy the antics of the red squirrels at our bird feeder, and we admire the stark beauty of tree trunks and shadows and snow crystals. We

Red squirrel at backyard feeder, Edmonton

check out animal tracks in the snow, and if we are lucky, we catch a glimpse of a coyote, deer or jack rabbit. It is the experience of reconnecting with the natural world, of which we are a part, that really counts.

We hope you find this guide helpful. There are many other more specialized and detailed resources to help you pursue an interest in birds, and we have identified some of these at the end of the book.

HARRY STELFOX
A wildlife biologist with Alberta Environmental Protection, Harry has pursued an interest in birds from the time he was a teenager growing up in the Lacombe area. As coordinator of Alberta's Watchable Wildlife Program (1988-1993) and vice-president/president of the Edmonton Natural History Club (1994-1997), he was the driving force in the production of the *Alberta Wildlife Viewing Guide* and *Nature Walks & Sunday Drives 'Round Edmonton*.

Boreal owl

CHAPTER TWO

EDMONTON IN WINTER—RED HOT FOR BIRDS?

Gordon Court

When one thinks of great winter birding hotspots, locations like Texas or Florida spring to mind. However, if one goes by the American Birding Association's "Most Wanted To See List" of birds, then Edmonton rates right up there with the best of them. Four of the top ten "Most Wanted" can be seen in the Edmonton area in winter. These four, all raptors (birds of prey), are boreal owl, northern hawk owl, gyrfalcon and great gray owl.

All of these species have been seen on the same day on a number of city of Edmonton Christmas Bird Counts. Boreal owls have been found in Whitemud Ravine and are occasionally detected near bird feeders in urban areas. These small, square-headed owls are often made obvious by the mobbing behaviour of chickadees and jays.

Northern hawk owls have a hawk-like posture and flight pattern. They are irruptive visitors to the Edmonton area, meaning some years they may be present and accounted for, in other years not seen at all. Wabamun Lake and the Opal pine forest are common locations for northern hawk owls when they are around.

Gyrfalcons nest in the Arctic, but winter wandering brings them south. Several gyrfalcons frequent the Edmonton area during winter, and some roost on city buildings during the evening. One adult male gyrfalcon, as of 1998, had roosted four years in a row on the Alberta Grain Terminals building in the northern part of the city. Birding alerts on the Bird Hotline (403-433-2473) have made this gyrfalcon one of the most frequently observed members of its species, ever!

Great gray owls, with their very round facial discs, are the largest of our winter owls. Although they have been observed within the city limits in winter, one usually has to be prepared to do some driving to see them. In good years (when the birds are seen regularly), they can be found during the day at Wabamun Lake, Elk Island National Park and in the pine forests and farmland near Opal and Redwater. The recent winter of 1996-97 was the most spectacular winter on record for this species in Alberta. In that season, up to 6 great grays were seen at one time at locations within an hour's drive of the city, and daily totals of over 20 individuals sighted were not uncommon.

Gyrfalcon

GORDON COURT

Gordon has been enjoying birds since he was a toddler and had most of his formative ornithological experiences while growing up in Edmonton. He has researched avian species in Alberta, the Canadian Arctic, Antarctica and New Zealand, but photographing birds has always been one of his greatest challenges and interests. He is happy to have contributed some of the photos used in this book. Gordon works as the provincial wildlife status biologist with Alberta Environmental Protection.

CHAPTER THREE

BIRDING IN THE BACKYARD

Ellen Scott

A youngster fills a backyard feeder,
Sherwood Park

Every living creature has three basic needs for survival: water, food and shelter. Most people living in the Edmonton region have running water, and nearby grocery stores for food, and live in buildings that provide shelter and heat. If any of these amenities were taken away, it is possible people could die of thirst, starvation or exposure. We often take for granted what we have; yet, there are many creatures in the wild that must expend a lot of energy to look for water, forage for food and find shelter. Facing the elements and meeting the three basic needs for survival is a difficult task for birds that live in the harsh conditions of the Edmonton region winter.

Water is vital to all of our overwintering birds. It is needed for body growth and maintenance, and for keeping clean. Feathers are designed to be wonderful insulators: interlocking shafts contain a lot of air and trap a bird's body heat very efficiently. But if feathers get dirty, the system breaks down, and the bird then becomes vulnerable to the cold. So, on warm, sunny days, even if the temperature is below freezing, birds will seek out puddles, gutters and other open water areas to bathe. Afterwards, they will spend a lot of time preening, fluffing their feathers back up and replacing the protective oils that help the feathers stay clean.

Spruce trees in Grandview Heights
back alley, Edmonton

The availability of food is another serious matter in winter, and bird feeders and backyard planting can greatly assist birds in their daily foraging.

Some birds, like finches and house sparrows, tend to eat first thing in the morning and again toward dusk. They can store a lot of food in their gullets, and while they sleep overnight, the food is slowly moved through their digestive system.

Other birds, such as chickadees, nuthatches, woodpeckers and jays, stash food in various hiding places for later use. This behaviour can begin as early as midsummer, so it is not uncommon in July or August to see a jay covering a peanut with a leaf in the centre of the lawn. Crotches of trees, leaf litter and residential flower planters are other hiding places used. Jays, in particular, have a remarkable memory for where they've stashed their food and can retrieve their tidbits up to a year later.

Birds find shelter in spruce trees, other coniferous cover, brush piles, hedgerows and, for species such as the redpolls and gray partridge, even snow drifts. Snow-laden spruce trees offer particularly excellent cover. When several birds roost next to a tree trunk, the ambient air temperature around them can rise significantly, even if it is -30°C outside. Cavity-nesting birds, such as chickadees, nuthatches and woodpeckers, roost overnight in tree cavities, sometimes huddling together for warmth. Chickadees emerging after a long winter's night look pretty ruffled and are not their usual, trim-looking selves.

White-tailed deer at hopper feeder, Edmonton

To attract a good number and diversity of birds to your backyard for winter viewing, you must provide these three basics of life: water, food and shelter. Your ability to do so will be affected by your determination to get information and prepare properly for the birds. The variety of birds that appear will also be influenced by the quality of habitat in the surrounding area. What features does your neighbourhood or area have that will attract birds, and what birds do you think it can attract?

How to provide water

There are several ways to provide water for overwintering birds. By supplying this scarce necessity, you will be giving the birds an added boost that will go a long way toward ensuring their survival over the long Edmonton area winter.

One way is to use a commercial birdbath heater. Many of these are submersible and have a built-in thermostat to improve energy efficiency. Some people have designed their own heaters, using light bulbs or old electric frying pans to heat their birdbaths.

Another way to provide water is to use a shallow, plastic basin or garbage pail lid.

The basin or lid can be filled with warm water and placed in a sunny area, such as a south-facing exposure against a dark fence. Putting the basin about a metre away from nearby shrubbery will give the birds cover for preening and protect them from predators. If you provide water in this manner daily, and at specific times, the birds will get used to the schedule and gratefully take advantage of your offering.

Some people worry about birds bathing in frigid temperatures. It is good to remember: a bird must be clean to stay warm. If feathers get dirty and matted, they will not be able to fluff up and hold air—for birds, the best insulator of all. So trust the birds; they know what they're doing. After all, they've been surviving in this climate for thousands of years.

Food and feeders

Each bird species has somewhat different food requirements and feeding behaviours that need to be considered in attracting them to an Edmonton area backyard in winter. (See chart on the next page.)

At bird feeders you can offer a variety of nuts and seeds, and you can hang or attach suet to a backyard tree. Through backyard planting you can attract birds with many different kinds of berries (e.g., mountain ash, dogwood, high-bush cranberry and saskatoon). Trees and bushes will also be a source of dormant insects, and insect larvae and eggs.

The key is variety—the greater the variety of foods you have in your yard, the more species you are likely to attract.

WINTER BIRD FEEDING CHART

Bird Species	Striped Sunflower	Black Sunflower	Millet	Corn	Peanuts	Niger	Suet	Feeder Type
Ruffed grouse, gray partridge and pheasant	2 (hulled)	2 (hulled)	1	1 (cracked)				platform (on ground)
Rock dove			1	1				platform (on ground)
Downy and hairy woodpecker	2						1	suet, platform (raised), hopper
Blue jay	2	3		3	1		2	platform (raised or on ground), hopper (sturdy)
Magpie	3				1		2	platform (raised or on ground)
Chickadees	2	1			1 (shelled)		2	hopper, tube, platform (raised), suet
Nuthatches		2			2 (shelled)		1	hopper, tube, platform (raised), suet
Starling	1	2		3	1 (crushed)		2	platform (on ground), suet
Junco		3	1	3		2	3	platform (on ground)
House sparrow	3 (hulled)		1	3			3	platform (raised or on ground), hopper
Pine siskin		2				1		tube, platform (raised or on ground), hopper
White-winged crossbill		3 (hulled)						platform (raised), hopper
Pine and evening grosbeak	1	2						platform (raised or on ground), hopper
Redpolls		1	3			1		platform (raised or on ground), hopper, tube

LEGEND: **1** - highly preferred   •   **2** - preferred   •   **3** - will eat

For instance, sunflower seeds will attract chickadees, grosbeaks, finches, jays and magpies, among others. Bohemian waxwings will be attracted to mountain ash berries; pine siskins and redpolls, to niger seeds; and the woodpeckers, nuthatches and golden-crowned kinglets, to suet.

Birds also have different feeding styles. Blue jays, magpies, ruffed grouse, gray partridge and ring-necked pheasant are large, ungainly birds that need solid footing to feed. These birds all forage on the ground and are best fed at ground-feeding stations, although the jays and magpies, being more agile, can easily feed at (and dominate) raised platform feeders.

Smaller ground feeders, like the dark-eyed junco and snow bunting, like to scratch out a living in the leaf litter and shallow snow but will sometimes visit ground-feeding stations.

Chickadees, nuthatches and finches, such as the common redpoll and pine siskin, will feed from platform and hanging feeders. All these birds are very acrobatic and can contort into the oddest positions when trying to reach their food.

The chickadees, nuthatches and jays will usually grab a seed or nut and take it away to a safe place before pecking it open. Then they will fly back for another food item. Finches, native sparrows and house sparrows usually stay at the feeder, cracking open the seeds with a grinding action of their beaks.

Woodpeckers and nuthatches like to forage along tree trunks, feeding on insects under the bark. Because it simulates these birds' natural food and feeding position, suet hung on a vertical surface will entice these birds to eat.

Bird food

Wild bird stores offer a great number of foods for backyard birds, and different seeds can be mixed according to the species you wish to attract. The most sought-after foods include striped sunflower seed, black oil (or black) sunflower seed, niger (the seed of a tropical thistle), white

GORDON COURT
Hopper feeder with common redpoll

millet, canola, peanuts (either shelled or unshelled), corn and suet mixtures. See the accompanying feeding chart to see what kind of food different bird species prefer.

Suet is the hard fat found around the heart and kidneys of sheep and cattle; regular fat is found throughout these animals' bodies and can be had by trimming meat cuts. Suet, in this book, includes both sources of fat. Purchased suet mixtures are usually rendered and have a little extra seed, ground peanuts or even fruit thrown in.

Making your own suet is relatively easy. You start with lard or vegetable shortening and mix in whatever you have on hand. Crushed peanuts, raisins, whole wheat flour, corn meal and sunflower seeds are great additions. Just mix your ingredients until you have a good, stiff consistency. Then put your concoction in muffin tins to form it into bird-sized chunks. Use a mesh bag (e.g., an onion bag) for a holder, put in your hardened treats, and tie the bag against a tree trunk. Any unused suet blocks can be stored in the freezer.

Bird feeders

Feeders come in different sizes, shapes and designs. However, all feeders are a variation of three different styles: hopper, platform and tube. Each of these styles serves slightly different functions and attracts different species of birds.

Hopper feeders. These feeders are usually wooden with a V-shaped container that slowly releases seed to the birds. This style is good for most birds and, when filled with black sunflower seeds, will attract chickadees, nuthatches, pine siskins and redpolls. If there is a sturdy landing platform and the feeder is stable, jays will also come to feed at a hopper. This type of feeder is usually hung from a tree or something else solid. However and wherever it is attached, a hopper feeder can't be allowed to swing too much or the seed will spill and the birds will be discouraged from visiting.

Platform feeders. The platform feeder is probably the best all-round, multi-purpose feeder. This feeder type consists primarily of an open or covered tray. It is usually mounted on a pole, giving it stability. If you put peanuts and sunflower seeds on it, it will become the

JOHN ACORN
Platform feeder with black-billed magpie

main bird feeder in a yard, with chickadees, blue jays, magpies, finches and house sparrows. If this feeder is mounted a metre and a half from the ground and about a metre from shrubbery, the birds will have some protection. Chickadees will be able to fly in, grab a seed, and fly to nearby cover to eat. Birds will not come to a feeder if they feel exposed and vulnerable.

Some platform feeders are designed to go on the ground (ground-feeding station). This style of feeder is used to attract house sparrows, juncos, pheasants, gray partridge and ruffed grouse. Again, protection is paramount. Place the feeder near a brush pile, shrubbery and/or a spruce tree to offer these birds the security they need.

If a platform feeder is not covered, snow and meltwater can be a problem. The best kinds of platform feeders have screen bottoms that allow drainage. Others have wooden bottoms with a lot of small holes drilled in them to encourage water flow. Snow should be brushed off as soon as possible. There is nothing worse than chipping away at a dried mush of millet and cracked corn. And from the birds' point of view, dining someplace that encourages mould and disease is probably not a good idea.

Tube feeders. Tube feeders are usually plastic and come shaped like tubes, balls and even pyramids or cubes. Fill these specialty feeders with black sunflower or niger seed (depending on the hole size), and the redpolls and pine siskins will be in seventh heaven. Black sunflower seeds and peanuts will also attract chickadees and nuthatches. Placing small tube feeders throughout the yard, against tree trunks or other vertical surfaces, will appeal to these birds' feeding style. Just don't fill a tube feeder with an all-purpose mix. House sparrows and finches

GORDON COURT

Tube feeder with pine siskins

will appreciate your efforts, but no other species will.

Making your own feeder

Feeders do not have to be fancy or expensive, although if you want to build something a little more complicated, there are lots of books that can tell you how (see *Recommended Reading* at the end of this book). Basically, the main requirements of a functional feeder are accessibility, a way of keeping the food dry, and drainage. You are limited only by your imagination.

A simple feeder that children can make requires a 2-L milk carton. Cut out a large opening in one or two sides of the carton, about 5 cm from the bottom. Poke a few small holes in the bottom for drainage, fill with black sunflower seeds, hang in a tree, and voilà, you have the perfect chickadee feeder.

Another way to involve children is to take large pine or spruce cones and smear them with peanut butter. The cones can then be tied with a piece of ribbon or string to a tree branch close to the trunk. These feeders are ideal for chickadees, nuthatches and woodpeckers. Some people mix the peanut butter with corn meal in the mistaken belief that the corn meal will prevent the peanut butter from sticking to the bird's digestive system. Birds don't have a problem digesting peanut butter, but the corn meal does make the peanut butter go further and adds some nutritional value.

Boreal chickadee at feeder with peanut butter

For another easy-to-make feeder, all you need is an old screen window. The screen provides the drainage, so you don't need to cover this feeder. Place it horizontally on bricks, fill it with millet and corn, and you have a fine feeder for sparrows, grouse and other ground-feeding birds. Just brush off the snow after a storm.

Wild bird stores and some nature centres also carry a variety of feeders for those of you not inclined to make your own.

Shelter

Not only is it good to offer water and food to overwintering birds, but also shelter. When planning and planting a bird-friendly garden, go native. Native trees and shrubs offer both shelter and food for birds, and can be attractive as well. For instance, dogwood provides both cover, and berries for food, and with its golds and reds, is very colourful in winter.

When designing your garden, think of what birds need to survive. Every bird has different habitat requirements. Some, like house sparrows, prefer hedges and spruce trees, whereas others, such as juncos, prefer brush piles. (A brush pile can easily be made with prunings from trees and shrubs.) A yard that has an open area and perennial stubble, graduating to shrubbery, then mature deciduous and coniferous trees, provides excellent, small-scale habitat. Spruce trees supply particularly good protection for roosting birds.

Remember to think like a bird when you are locating your feeders or birdbaths. The birds need to be safe from predators—the flying type, as well as the four-legged and two-legged types. Putting a feeder or birdbath a few feet from a shrub is a good rule of thumb. Then the birds can land, check the area and flee if they sense danger. Placing bird stations close but not too close to bushes is particularly useful for cutting down on cat attacks. Since many cats like to pounce from cover, having some open space between a shrub and where the birds are helps remove the cat's advantage.

If you provide all the elements of water, food and shelter in your backyard, you have more than a reasonable chance of seeing a broad cross-section of birds during the winter months. Some years are better than others, though, because we can't always rely on species like the redpolls, pine siskins or crossbills to show up. So plant your garden, put out your suet and seeds and see what comes. Good luck!

ELLEN SCOTT

Ellen grew up in the bush of northern Ontario, where her love of birds and natural history was nurtured by both her surroundings and her father and grandfather. In 1989, with her father, Jack Clements, Ellen started *The Wildbird General Store*, a specialty shop in Edmonton for birdwatchers. She has since gone on to other projects, including writing about ecotourism on the Internet.

CHAPTER FOUR

FROST-FREE BIRDING TIPS

Dave Ealey

Two stylish winter birders, 1996 Strathcona Christmas Bird Count, temperature -30°C

Many Edmonton birders, once the first snow flies, pack away their binoculars, close up their notebooks and file away their bird guides until the following spring. What a shame! They miss out on a significant period in the lives of our resident birds, not to mention the special feathered visitors we see only during our winters.

These fair-weather birdwatchers have a litany of excuses: it's too cold, my binoculars freeze up, and there aren't enough birds to make it worthwhile. Nonsense! With a little preparation and planning, winter birding can be both fun and informative. Tips from winter birding enthusiasts can help both the rookie and warm-weather expert apply tried-and-true field techniques, perhaps even add to our knowledge of winter birds, all the while staying reasonably warm and comfortable.

Some basics

The first step is to decide what the focus of your birding trip is going to be. How you approach winter birding depends tremendously on your objectives for the day. Do you want to study a particular species? Do you want to get to know what birds stay in certain habitats? Are you interested in following changes in bird activity in a specific area over time?

To study the activities of birds of a certain species, you'll have to be prepared to follow when they move, yet stay still (and warm!) when watching from close quarters. Thoroughly surveying a particular habitat for any and all birds will require frequent traverses at a number of different portions of the habitat—you might just need a map and compass to avoid getting lost.

Edmonton's short winter days, with no more than seven hours of daylight around December 21, make it difficult to plan long trips. Luckily, there are numerous locations in and around the city that you can easily reach by car and return in a few hours. Chapter 5 gives you tips on where you can find some of the most important locations for winter birds in the Edmonton region.

Safety first

The short days and winter conditions do require that birders plan safe trips. Winter birding trips are safer when shared, especially if you plan to hike, ski or snowshoe any distance from your vehicle. The margin for error is slimmer in winter, so it pays to carry a small survival kit on extended hikes (probably not a bad idea for any time of year).

Obviously there is little point in birding during truly extreme conditions—when a blizzard is blowing, temperatures are below -20°C, or driving conditions are treacherous. The birds tend to be less active in really cool weather, so you'd have a much harder time finding them anyway. In addition, they are more vulnerable to the effects of disturbance in such conditions, so it is unwise to intrude on them. But things like deep snow, shallow sunlight that can be blinding or create significant shade, and temperatures between -20°C and +5°C are no problem for the prepared birder.

The stylish winter birder

Even if most of your birding consists of very short jaunts away from your vehicle, which is quite common during Christmas Bird Counts for example, you still have to keep warm. So, unlike Edmonton's Christmas Bird Count mascot, masterfully penned by Yardley Jones, the well-dressed birder must forget about being stylish. (There's nothing stylish about frostbite!)

Warm, loose-fitting clothing is ideal, several layers being better than skimpy clothing beneath a heavy down coat. Longer coats, about three-quarter length, are better than waist-length jackets. This way of dressing gives the birder the insulating advantage of air trapped in clothes, much like the down-and-feather covering of birds. On very cold days, birds fluff their feathers to trap insulating air, which makes them look as much as twice their normal size.

Loose clothing also allows moisture to work its way out from your body, rather than condense and freeze as it would with tight-fitting clothing.

Keep your extremities covered and warm—head, fingers and toes. Whatever you choose to wear on your head, whether a toque, fur hat, hood or scarf, always remember that a significant portion of your body heat escapes through your head and the back of your neck. Protect yourself from this considerable heat loss! And when wearing binoculars, you will find that high-collar shirts and sweaters work better than scarves.

Binoculars are cold to hold, but mittens make focusing difficult—thin wool gloves inside mitts allow you to focus when you have to but also let you keep your hands warm between sightings.

Winter boots with good insulation and tall sides that can be sealed off with gaiters are ideal for heavy slogging through the snow. Skis or snowshoes, unless the snow is exceptionally deep, are often a hindrance when you follow birds through the bush.

An army of birders marches on its stomach

When planning your birding trip, don't forget to pack food and a hot drink, or make plans to refuel yourself along the way. Since the beginning of Edmonton birders' efforts to secure the title of Biggest Christmas Bird Count in the World, replenishing the body during the day and the potluck supper finale have proven key to sustaining enthusiasm. Most of the birding teams on Christmas Bird Count day get an early start and gather at 24-hour donut shops or other fast food restaurants.

Edmonton area owl prowler

Some of Edmonton's renowned "owl prowlers" rely on a diet of coffee and donuts to make it through a long night of owl censusing.

The tools of the trade

Viewing birds during winter means using your birding equipment correctly and learning how to detect birds more effectively. A good pair of binoculars is a birder's most indispensable tool. Using binoculars in winter can be a tricky job—they are prone to fogging and can be hard to focus because of stiffness caused by the cold.

Preventing fogging of lenses on your binoculars means keeping moist air from condensing on cold lenses. Holding binoculars just slightly away from your face while you look through the eyepieces will help keep the lenses from fogging. Avoid breathing toward the binoculars. Anti-fogging cleansers used for eyeglasses can be helpful on your binoculars, but don't expect their effect to last very long. A soft cloth for removing frost is a useful addition to your field equipment and should be kept

Now where did that pileated woodpecker go?

clean and handy in an external pocket. Thoroughly sealed binocular frames are less likely to give you problems with condensation within the binoculars themselves.

When walking, it helps to keep your binoculars tucked just inside a loose fold of your coat—they can be ready in a moment, yet kept warm enough that focusing is not too stiff. Focusing levers (on so-called thumb-focus binoculars) or large focusing wheels make it easier for gloved hands to adjust an image. Metallic-bodied binoculars are much colder to operate than those with a moulded exterior. Consider getting binoculars that can be used in any weather.

Bird detection

Binoculars are useless unless you have something to observe. Detecting birds during the winter is often difficult because they rarely sing and are very busy, both foraging for food and keeping warm in sheltered areas. The solution to bird detection at this time of year is to stop, look, listen and "pish." Improve your chances of identifying birds on bright, sunny days by approaching birds from the sunward side.

Stop

The low angle of light on sunny winter days means there will be low-light conditions and lots of shade, making the birds hard to spot. Make frequent stops, either walking or driving, to give yourself a chance to inspect the habitat from all angles. In addition, when you stop, the noise of the car or your footsteps on the snow will no longer drown out the thin calls that many of our small flocking birds make as they move about in winter. Although cars make good blinds when watching birds, the sides of roads in winter may not be safe for pulling over—use caution when stopping.

Look

Scan frequently for sudden movement or to catch a glimpse of a flying bird. Across large open areas, you will have a better chance of detecting a perched bird if you take the time to sweep the horizon with your binoculars or spotting scope. Things that look like birds, such as tattered wasp nests, dead leaves attached to twigs, and assorted garbage, can make for a frustrating outing. Learn to separate this flotsam from the true bird silhouette by noting the locations among tree branches that perched birds usually occupy.

Listen

Foraging flocks of chickadees, pine siskins or crossbills, among others, are frequently calling as they flit through an area. Stay alert for these often high-pitched sounds. All it takes is one bird to call and you may be able to spot an entire flock. Many birdwatchers identify the birds they come across by the call note alone. You may also hear the tapping of a woodpecker chiseling through bark to its next meal. Rarely, you will hear small or medium-sized birds join in a raucous chorus as they mob a large hawk or owl.

DAVE EALEY

A professional biologist/editor/communicator, Dave developed an interest in birds through school projects when he was a young student in England. Serious birding didn't emerge until his undergraduate years in Kingston, Ontario, where he first took part in a Christmas Bird Count. Many years later, Dave enjoys organizing and taking part in bird surveys of all kinds, as well as lending his hand to publishing projects that promote the study of Alberta's birds.

Pish

If the birds seem absent from good woodland habitat, despite your scanning and listening efforts, you may be able to attract them by "squeaking" or "pishing." Flocks of chickadees, sometimes accompanied by other small species, are often attracted by these sounds. Squeaking is created by placing a wet "kiss" on the back of an ungloved hand and loudly sucking in air. If the day is particularly cold, pishing is easier to do; it consists of almost spitting out the word "pish" repeatedly. The emphasis is on the "shhh" sound, and it is anything but quiet. If the birds are within hearing distance, they will soon respond to these noises with their own call notes.

Is birding in the winter worth all this effort? Our northern winters are an integral part of many birds' existence. Over the years, 120 species have been recorded in the Edmonton region during winter, including 15 species that are rarely seen outside the winter period. Birds have developed energy-conserving behaviours, such as social roosting, and certain birds can be more conspicuous during the winter than during the breeding season, when foliage obscures their activities.

Can inexperienced birders enjoy winter birding? Winter is an excellent time for new birders to develop their skills. There aren't as many species around in winter, so with fewer birds to choose from, identification is easier. And if you learn your birds in winter, you'll be a step ahead in identifying those that remain in the region in the summer.

Despite some discomfort, winter birding in the field has its own fascinations and ability to enlighten. And besides, for the true birding enthusiast, it's a long time between October and April. It would be a shame to be an armchair birder for the entire period.

CHAPTER FIVE

EDMONTON REGION HABITATS AND VIEWING LOCATIONS

Harry Stelfox

Successful birdwatching, at any time of the year, requires some knowledge of what areas are likely to harbour different bird species at different seasons. Just like people, birds are attracted to areas that provide a suitable home environment or habitat. Of course, the conditions that provide food and shelter vary from one bird species to another, depending on their special adaptations and preferences. For example, in winter, gray partridge are attracted to weedy field and low shrub areas that provide seeds for food, plus dense grass and shrubs for shelter and protection from predators. In contrast, black-capped chickadees prefer deciduous and mixedwood forest, as well as mature residential areas, where they have shelter and can also find small insects in the bark of trees, along with the suet and seeds provided by homeowners.

Birds often frequent different habitats at different times of the year and their behaviours will also change with the season. For instance, in winter, the Bohemian waxwing forms large foraging flocks that seek out the fruit of the mountain ash and other ornamental trees and shrubs found mainly in urban residential areas. During the spring, the flocks disperse, and the birds migrate north to the boreal forest, where breeding pairs nest and raise their young.

By learning about the winter habitat preferences of different bird species and where those habitats can be found, you will greatly increase your success in seeing, learning about and enjoying winter resident birds. You will also learn that some areas have more productive and diverse habitats that support larger numbers of birds as well as a greater diversity of species. These areas could be considered winter birding "hot spots" and are well known by local birders. Several of these hot spots are identified under the habitat types treated in the remainder of the chapter.

The following material is organized by five major habitat types that occur in the Edmonton region, namely, coniferous and mixedwood forest, deciduous forest, field/shelterbelt complex, open water and mature residential. For each habitat type there is a description of its main characteristics, the common winter resident birds that are likely to occur there and some of the best places for searching out these habitats and their associated bird species. We also provide maps of both the city of Edmonton and Edmonton region to assist you in getting to these locations. (See page 16.)

Many of the destinations referred to in this chapter are described in more detail in *Nature Walks & Sunday Drives 'Round Edmonton*. This book, also published by the Edmonton Natural History Club, includes more detailed maps showing how to access each viewing site.

Coniferous and mixedwood forest

This habitat type is characterized by treed areas dominated by mature coniferous species. Coniferous means that the trees are cone-bearing; native conifers of the Edmonton region are all needle-leaved.

The most common native coniferous tree in the Edmonton region is white spruce, which prefers cool, moist sites created by the shade of other trees, as well as north-facing hillsides, valley slopes and protected ravines. Three other less

Great gray owl in mature coniferous forest near Newbrook, north of Redwater

common native conifer species are jack pine, black spruce and tamarack. Jack pine is found in sandy areas, whereas black spruce and tamarack are associated with wet, poorly drained peatland locations. These conifer species are particularly well adapted to the long, cold winters of our northern boreal forests, as are associated bird species like the gray jay, great gray owl and common raven.

Most conifer species are evergreen, meaning that they retain their leaves (i.e., needles) throughout the year. Tamarack is an exception to the rule, turning golden yellow in the fall before dropping its needles. Evergreen trees are very attractive to many bird species because they provide an excellent refuge from cold, stormy weather, as well as protection from predators, when most other trees are stripped of their leaves. The dense, needle-covered branches of white and black spruce provide important shelter for species like black-capped chickadee, blue jay, red-breasted nuthatch and dark-eyed junco. The branches of these conifers also catch and hold fluffy layers of snow that provide additional thermal cover.

Another key aspect of coniferous trees is that they produce cones that contain seeds that are an important winter food source for birds such as the white-winged crossbill. In addition, the rough, flaky bark on the trunks and larger branches of conifers provides a winter refuge for many insects. These insects, in turn, are

an important source of food for golden-crowned kinglets, three-toed woodpeckers, as well as the red-breasted nuthatch and brown creeper.

White spruce forests tend to be relatively old (e.g., 80 to 150 years old) because this spruce grows slowly and is successional to (follows and replaces) deciduous trees. For this reason, white spruce are often associated with large deciduous trees, as well as standing, dead deciduous snags and fallen logs. This complex structure adds diversity to the forest and makes it attractive to a large variety of wildlife. When conifers and deciduous trees are found together, the woodland is called a mixedwood forest. In these areas, keep an eye out for pileated woodpecker and white-breasted nuthatch, both of which are attracted to the large, old poplar trees.

Good examples of coniferous and mixedwood habitat in the Edmonton region can be found along the north-facing slopes of the North Saskatchewan River valley and the steep-sided ravines that feed into the river valley. Within the city of Edmonton, check out the hiking trails on the south side of the river between the LRT Bridge and Groat Bridge, between William Hawrelak Park and the Whitemud Equine Centre, plus the lower sections of the Whitemud Ravine.

Mixedwood forest at mouth of Whitemud Creek—looking at Laurier Heights, Edmonton

CITY OF EDMONTON AND EDMONTON REGION
WINTER BIRD-VIEWING SITES

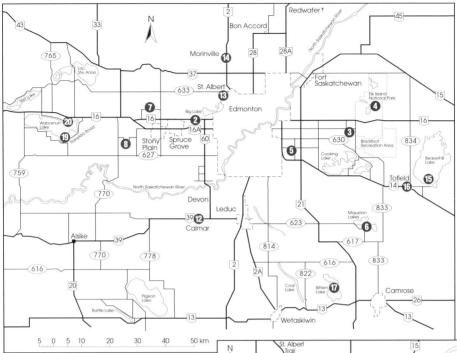

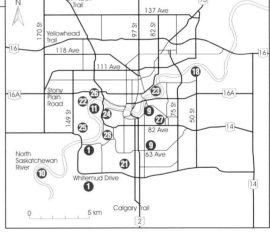

Coniferous and Mixedwood Forest
1 - Whitemud Ravine
2 - Wagner Natural Area
3 - Strathcona Wilderness Centre
4 - Elk Island National Park

Deciduous Forest
1 - Whitemud Ravine
4 - Elk Island National Park
5 - Sherwood Park Natural Area
6 - Miquelon Lake Provincial Park
7 - Chickakoo Lake Recreation Area
8 - Hasse Lake Provincial Park
9 - Mill Creek Ravine
10 - Terwillegar Park
11 - William Hawrelak Park

Field/Shelterbelt Complex
12 - Calmar
13 - St. Albert
14 - Morinville
15 - Beaverhill Lake
16 - Tofield
17 - Bittern Lake

Open Water
10 - Terwillegar Park
18 - Goldbar Park
19 - Keephills and Sundance Power Plants
20 - Wabamun Townsite

Mature Residential
21 - Pleasantview Cemetery
22 - Crestwood
23 - Riverdale
24 - Windsor Park
25 - Laurier Heights
26 - Glenora
27 - Bonnie Doon
28 - Belgravia

Black-capped chickadee

Outside of the city, Wagner Natural Area along Highway 16 West, Strathcona Wilderness Centre east of Sherwood Park, and parts of Elk Island National Park (including treed islands in Astotin Lake, which have not been subjected to wildfire for many decades) provide good birding opportunities in this habitat type.

Deciduous forest

Deciduous trees, which shed their leaves in the fall, characterize this habitat type. The most common native deciduous tree species are aspen, balsam poplar and white birch. Aspen typically forms dense, even-aged stands in upland sites. This tree is adapted to sprout new stems quickly from its roots if disturbed by fire or clearing. Balsam poplar and birch prefer moist and wet sites in river valleys, ravines and boggy areas. These last two tree species are often found in association with spruce trees.

Deciduous forest in Strathcona County

Deciduous trees are generally shorter-lived than conifer trees, and after 50 to 70 years, you will commonly find standing dead trees and fallen logs on the forest floor. Snags and large logs provide a smorgasbord of wood-boring insects that are eaten by the crow-sized pileated woodpecker, as well as the much smaller hairy and downy woodpeckers. On a calm, cold winter day, listen for the tapping and chipping sound of woodpeckers in a mature deciduous forest. Nest cavities created by woodpeckers in both live and dead trees provide important shelter and roosting sites for small birds like chickadees; here they can huddle together and protect themselves against the cold. The northern saw-whet owl roosts during the winter in the larger nest cavities created by the pileated woodpecker.

Sunlight is able to penetrate the canopy (upper branches) of deciduous forests better than that of coniferous forests. As a result, there is usually a well-developed understory of herbaceous (non-woody) ground cover and shrubs in deciduous forest, which provides insects, berries and seeds as food sources for such winter residents as ruffed grouse, black-capped chickadee, dark-eyed junco and pine grosbeak. Deciduous forests also attract predatory bird species such as northern goshawk, great horned owl, northern saw-whet owl and great gray owl because here they are able to find food in the form of small rodents, snowshoe hares, ruffed grouse and other bird species.

Forests with birch trees are particularly attractive to common redpolls, which feed on the tiny seeds embedded in the small oblong seed catkins found at the tips of this tree's branches. Redpolls breed in the northern boreal forest and taiga but move south during winter in foraging flocks of several dozen or even hundreds of individuals. A telltale sign of their presence is a dusting of tiny orange-brown scales on the snow beneath some birches.

There are numerous deciduous forest sites that are excellent for winter birdwatching, both within the city of Edmonton and in surrounding areas. Many of these sites have good hiking trails, and depending on snow conditions, cross-country skiing provides an excellent way to get around. Sites to explore east of the city include Sherwood Park Natural Area, Miquelon Lake Provincial Park and Elk Island National Park. West of the city, check out Chickakoo Lake Recreation Area

Shelterbelt east of Millet

and Hasse Lake Provincial Park. Within Edmonton, Mill Creek Ravine, Whitemud Ravine, Terwillegar Park and William Hawrelak Park, all have deciduous forest and associated winter bird life.

Field/shelterbelt complex

This habitat type is characterized by farmland with its relatively barren, snow-covered fields; these open country areas often include small patches of trees and shrub-ringed wetland depressions or potholes. Some fields are bordered by narrow strips of trees, shrubs and dense grass along fencelines and roadside ditches. Farmsteads or acreage residences often have a well-developed complex of planted trees and shrubs forming perimeter shelterbelt vegetation around the buildings.

Open field habitat near Rivière Qui Barre, west of Morinville

In winter, open field habitat provides limited food and cover for birds. However, rodents that are active under the snow are of great interest to snowy owls and rough-legged hawks that have moved south from their Arctic breeding grounds in search of more abundant winter food supplies. Scavengers, such as black-billed magpie and common raven, also frequent these areas in search of carrion resulting from predator-killed, road-killed or winter-starved animals. Whirling flocks of seed-eating snow buntings are another less common sight in open fields in winter.

Shelterbelt habitat is characterized by a mixture of native and introduced trees and shrubs, prime winter habitat for a number of species, including black-capped chickadee, house sparrow, northern shrike, downy and hairy woodpeckers and black-billed magpie. Seed and fruit-bearing trees and shrubs, such as Manitoba maple, white and blue spruce, mountain ash, apple and crabapple, high-bush cranberry and cotoneaster, will also attract such birds as Bohemian waxwing, evening grosbeak, pine grosbeak and white-winged crossbill.

Waste grain around farmsteads and granaries provides an easy meal for house sparrows, rock doves (pigeons), gray partridge and European starlings.

Open field habitat with farmsteads is not hard to find as it dominates the landscape in the Edmonton region. Country residential acreages, which tend to have a high proportion of wooded shelterbelts, are prevalent in the hilly country of the Cooking Lake Moraine east of Edmonton, the Glory Hills north of Stony Plain, and the Sandhills region north of Devon. Most of this land is privately owned, so the best way to conduct your birding in such areas is to drive slowly down a country road, and when you sight a bird, pull over wherever it is safe to stop.

Very open field habitats that seem to be particularly attractive to snowy owls can be found just south of the city of Edmonton toward Leduc and Calmar, near Bittern Lake west of Camrose, and north of St. Albert in the Villeneuve and Morinville area. Open country around Beaverhill Lake north and east of Tofield is also good for snowies. Keep an eye out for these birds perched on top of telephone and power poles, as well as fence posts.

Wetland in Elk Island National Park

Small patches of aspen and balsam poplar woods, as well as shelterbelt complexes around abandoned farmsteads, are good places to spot great horned owls. Look for old hawk nests in the crotch of larger trees; they provide nesting sites for this owl species, which starts nesting in February.

Open water
During the middle of a typical winter in the Edmonton region, open water habitat is localized to a few areas where warm water discharge from power, water treatment and sewage treatment plants keeps the water surface ice-free. Waterfowl that stay too late in the fall become dependent on these sites. These few open water areas can provide sufficient food and resting habitat to support several dozen to a few hundred waterfowl in the city, several thousand in the Wabamun Lake area.

Mallard and common goldeneye are the most common species that overwinter in these areas. Mallards are able to supplement their aquatic diet with waste grain in farm fields when there is not too much snow cover, but common goldeneye are entirely aquatic in their feeding habits. Less common waterfowl species that can be found at this time of year include lesser scaup, Canada goose, common merganser and bufflehead.

Research on overwintering waterfowl has shown that many of them do not fare all that well. These birds can use more energy than they consume, losing a significant percentage of their body weight by late winter. They are then weak and vulnerable to predation.

Bald eagles typically follow the late fall waterfowl migration south. They find weak and injured waterfowl make easy pickings as the wetlands begin to freeze and the remaining birds are concentrated at the open water sites. Some of these eagles stay late enough to be counted on Christmas Bird Counts in the Edmonton region. They are often sighted cruising the open water habitats of the North Saskatchewan River and Wabamun Lake.

In the city of Edmonton during winter, open water habitat is found along the North Saskatchewan River at the following locations: below the E.L. Smith water treatment plant in the west end near Terwillegar Park, downstream from the Rossdale power and water treatment plant by the 105th Street Bridge, and downstream from the sewage treatment plant at Goldbar Park. Riverside foot trails and pedestrian foot bridges over the river provide good viewing opportunities. However, because the birds may be some distance out on the water, spotting scopes are recommended for close-up looks and to identify any rare or unusual species (e.g., yellow-billed loon) that may be hanging around.

Open water of North Saskatchewan River at Goldbar Park, Edmonton

The same applies to the Wabamun Lake sites west of the city. Extensive open water areas are associated with the TransAlta power plant by the Wabamun townsite, as well as the Keephills and Sundance power plants on the south shore of the lake. Access to these last areas is via the Wabamun Lake Provincial Park turnoff, which takes you south to the TransAlta Road (watch for directional signs). Keep your eyes open for bald eagles and gyrfalcons.

Mature residential

This habitat type is provided by older, well-landscaped urban and suburban areas that have an abundance of tall shrubs and trees. Generally, these areas are at least 25 to 30 years old, so many trees will extend well above the roof of a single-story house. A key characteristic of this habitat is the prevalence of ornamental trees (e.g., Colorado blue spruce, green ash, hybrid poplar, apple, crabapple and mountain ash) and shrubs/hedges (e.g., cotoneaster, Nanking cherry, lilac, currant and juniper), which intermix with buildings, streets, people, pets and cars. Small patches of native trees, shrubs and grassy areas are occasionally found in this habitat type.

Mature residential habitat of Edmonton's Belgravia neighbourhood

Mature residential habitat (along with the field/shelterbelt complex) attracts a lot of the house sparrows, rock doves (pigeons) and black-billed magpies found in winter in the Edmonton region. Warmth and cover are provided by the nooks and crannies of heated buildings, as well as clusters of large conifer trees and dense hedges. Human food sources include food scraps, pet food and the birdseed and suet supplied at backyard feeders (see Chapter 3). The food and cover provided by mature residential landscaping also attract the likes of black-capped chickadee, Bohemian waxwing, merlin, red- and white-breasted

nuthatches, downy and hairy woodpeckers, blue jay, pine siskin, common redpoll, white-winged and red crossbills, and European starling, as well as pine and evening grosbeaks.

Good examples of this habitat type can be found in the older sections of Edmonton and other communities in the region. Well-landscaped and older cemeteries also contribute habitat of this type and often provide excellent winter birding opportunities. The Pleasantview Cemetery at 106th Street and 53rd Avenue in Edmonton is a good example.

Mature residential areas that are near patches of natural forest habitat are likely to harbour larger and more diverse populations of winter bird species. Most of these neighbourhoods in Edmonton are found in proximity to the river valley and major ravines, and include Laurier Heights, Crestwood, Glenora, Riverdale, Bonnie Doon, Windsor Park and Belgravia.

Most of these older neighbourhoods have back alleys, and these are particularly good routes to hike for birdwatching—most feeders are in backyards, and also, some backyards have small, rough and wild corners that add habitat value. Highly manicured yards do not offer the same quality of winter food and cover for birds as those that are allowed to naturalize and have a good layering of low, medium and tall plant species.

Take some time to locate and become familiar with these habitat types, even before the winter season starts. By keeping lists of bird species observed by habitat, you will begin to appreciate the affinity that different birds have for specific habitat features and associated food and cover. It is this kind of information that is essential in efforts to conserve the habitats of our overwintering species. Even man-made habitats can be very beneficial.

CHAPTER SIX

A FEAST FOR THE EYES—WINTER BIRDS OF THE EDMONTON REGION

INTRODUCTION
Chris Fisher

This chapter provides descriptions and photographs of 32 of the most common birds that annually grace the Edmonton winter landscape. The descriptions are brief, stressing those features of appearance, character and behaviour that make each species notable and interesting.

The identification process is, with a few exceptions, moderately easy. In each species account there is some information to help with field identification, but it is not intended to be comprehensive. Several exceptional photographs accompany the species write-ups, and readers are encouraged to study them when attempting to identify the birds they see. Whole books have been written on Alberta's birds and bird identification, and the curious are referred to the bibliography at the end of this book.

Only those birds that are most likely to be seen during the Edmonton winter are given a full species account. By looking at Appendix 2, which categorizes and lists birds by their presence during the Edmonton region Christmas Bird Counts, you will see that all the species on the "A" list ("common or expected most years") have a full account or a good mention in another account. Many birds from the "B" list ("fairly common or of fairly regular occurrence") also have received attention; only a couple from the "C" list ("uncommon to rare") have been noted.

There are always a few species like the American robin, bald eagle or northern

GORDON COURT

Great horned owl

flicker that make irregular and surprise appearances. Their dependence on altered environments such as feeders, ornamental trees or open water to survive the winter means they will appear much more rarely than many of those hardy species written about here. We hope you will appreciate both the rarities and the regular winter visitors, whose survival skills can only earn them our deepest respect.

CHRIS FISHER
Chris has been keenly interested in the natural world as long as he can remember, and his graduate training at the University of Alberta has led him to many areas of great beauty and ecological interest across North America and Southeast Asia. Chris writes field guides (including the recent *Birds of Alberta*), lectures and leads field trips, all in the hope of inspiring others to embrace the natural world and its wonders.

GORDON COURT

Mallard

Anas platyrhynchos
Alan Hingston

The mallard is the familiar wild duck—the metallic green head and chestnut breast of the male being immediately recognizable. The female is an overall mottled brown, although the blue wing patch with white border distinguishes her from other duck species. Both male and female mallards *quack*, but when pairs are together, you will likely only hear the female.

Mallards are dabbling ducks, meaning they tip up to feed on bottom vegetation. In Edmonton, these ducks are often seen loafing or feeding at the edge of the river during winter, generally in slower-flowing open water areas, either downstream of waste water treatment plants (e.g., Goldbar) or the city power plant. Several thousand mallards overwinter in the Wabamun Lake area on cooling ponds at the Keephills and Sundance power plants; these ducks can also be viewed from the town pier in Wabamun, where heated water from the town power plant keeps part of the lake open all winter.

WAYNE LYNCH

Common Goldeneye

Bucephala clangula
Alan Hingston

Common goldeneyes are diving ducks—to feed, they submerge for several seconds before bobbing, cork-like, back to the surface.

The male common goldeneye is a striking black-and-white duck. In good light, the black head shows a green sheen, background to a large white spot and bright yellow eye. The female is generally gray, with a brown head and white flash along the flanks. In flight, the black-and-white pattern and swift flight of this duck are as distinctive as the whistling sound made by its wings.

In winter, loose flocks of these ducks can be found along the river in Edmonton, generally in faster-flowing open water areas warmed by effluent discharge, or in the vicinity of the Wabamun Lake power plants. In late winter, when there is still considerable ice on the water, male goldeneyes compete for females with animated "head-pointing" displays.

GORDON COURT

Northern Goshawk
Accipiter gentilis
Gordon Court

The northern goshawk is a handsome, but secretive, denizen of the forested regions of Alberta. In winter, this raptor wanders widely in search of food that may include species as large as the snowshoe hare. It usually watches for its prey from low perches, frequently on the edge of heavy bush. When detected in flight, it is frequently mistaken for a gyrfalcon; however, if it flies into the cover of trees, it is certainly a goshawk.

The back of an adult goshawk is beautifully marked with powder blue, although from below the bird appears gray, with fine barring on the breast and thighs. The eye colour varies from light orange to deep crimson. Juvenile birds are brown, with heavy streaking on the breast, and the eyes are light yellow. Both adult and young goshawks sport a distinctive white stripe over the eye, and their flight is the "flap-flap-glide" characteristic of all in the accipiter family.

Merlin
Falco columbarius
Gordon Court

The merlin is a common sight for Albertans, especially urbanites, as this dashing falcon is the most common raptor in the major cities of the province, summer and winter. In fact, Edmonton was recently proven to be the merlin capital of the world, with over 100 breeding pairs nesting in the city in 1995. Edmonton also holds the record for the most merlins ever recorded on a Christmas Bird Count, with 41 seen in 1986.

GORDON COURT

Merlins are small and dark, appearing slaty blue (males) or dusky brown (females). They are primarily bird predators and hunt "on the wing." With extremely fast, direct flight, they use their speed to surprise small songbirds and are particularly fond of house sparrows. When merlins remain in the city during winter, they also like to feed on Bohemian waxwings, which are attracted by the berry crops on the introduced mountain ash.

Gray partridge

EDGAR T. JONES

Ring-necked pheasant

EDGAR T. JONES

Ruffed grouse

JOHN ACORN

Gray Partridge
Perdix perdix

Ring-necked Pheasant
Phasianus colchicus

Ruffed Grouse
Bonasa umbellus

Alan Hingston

Although these three species of gamebirds are familiar to most observers, often our only view is of a single bird or small flock of chicken-like birds rising up explosively and vanishing quickly on whirring wings. The best way to differentiate between these species is by size, habitat and the tail of the rapidly disappearing bird. The gray partridge is a small, dumpy bird, almost always encountered in wide open stubble or ploughed fields. The larger pheasant is usually in woodlots or, if in fields, not far from cover. The ruffed grouse is almost always in deep aspen or mixedwood forest. If viewing permits, the long, pointed tail of the pheasant is diagnostic, and a careful observer should be able to detect the orange outer tail feathers of the gray partridge or the broad black band on the tail of the ruffed grouse.

Only the ruffed grouse is native to the province. Both the gray partridge and pheasant were introduced from Europe at the turn of the century, mainly for sport hunting. The numbers of all three species tend to fluctuate on a ten-year cycle that may be related to such factors as availability of food and abundance of predators.

Pheasant populations have been maintained by releasing hatchery-raised birds to replace those lost to hunting and high mortality during severe winters. However, figures from the Edmonton Christmas Bird Count indicate that pheasant as well as gray partridge and ruffed grouse have been declining over the past several years in the Edmonton area. All three species are probably victims of habitat loss, as farmland is increasingly used for housing and industrial developments. For those lucky people with houses or cabins backing onto ravines or fields, one or more of these species can be a surprise winter visitor, perhaps attracted by the spilled grain under a bird feeder.

RAY CROMIE

Rock Dove

Columba livia
Melanie Ostopowich

The rock dove, or domestic pigeon, is a species that is common all over Edmonton, even in winter. This introduced bird is often seen feeding on the ground—eating seeds, spilled grain or scattered garbage, and will visit ground-feeding stations. In turn, pigeons are a food source for overwintering birds of prey, such as merlins and gyrfalcons. The rock dove's distinctive call sounds like *k't'coo*, and the male's rolling courtship call resembles *oorook'tookoo*.

This bird is often selectively bred, so can come in many colours, ranging from all white to all black. However, it is most commonly seen with its normal wild plumage—blue-gray head, iridescent neck, light gray back and two dark wing bars. The pigeon is such a familiar sight that even beginning birdwatchers have little trouble identifying it. But it can sometimes be mistaken for other species: many a birdwatcher will admit to briefly mistaking a pigeon in flight for a small falcon.

Great Horned Owl

Bubo virginianus
Christine Rice

The piercing yellow glare of Alberta's provincial bird conveys its fearless nature. This silent stalker of night skies will seek out snowshoe hares, skunks and the occasional porcupine as prey, although typically it seems satisfied with meals of small mammals.

GORDON COURT

Great horned owls are very large (about 60 cm in length) and have distinct ear tufts and a white throat patch. However, it takes a keen eye to spot this common resident of Edmonton's wooded valleys because its finely barred, gray-brown feathers camouflage its presence during its daytime roosts. On winter evenings, you may see it outlined against a darkening sky or hear its familiar call—four to seven low-pitched hoots.

These owls are very early nesters, moving into the abandoned stick nests of hawks and crows in mid-February. By late March, it is not uncommon to see two to three newly hatched owlets peering above a snow-rimmed nest.

JOHN ACORN

Snowy Owl
Nyctea scandiaca
Lisa Takats

This regal winter visitor from the Arctic wears a sleek coat and boots of white feathers. Although all "snowies" are predominantly white, females have dark barring (chocolate brown to charcoal gray) over their body, and immature birds are even more heavily marked. The female snowy is one of the largest owls to be seen in Alberta in the winter (up to 64 cm in total length), with males considerably smaller.

With its elegant white face and distinctive yellow eyes, this day-hunting owl is seen most often on fence posts, hay bales, trees and power poles, from which it surveys the stubble fields for prey. It is drawn southward in winter to hunt our fields for small mammals and birds, but the numbers that arrive can be quite variable. Many birding trips are made exclusively to encounter this noble bird, whose yearly presence in the fields surrounding Edmonton makes many a naturalist's winter much more bearable.

Northern Saw-whet Owl
Aegolius acadicus
Lisa Takats

The quiet, tooting whistle of the northern saw-whet owl is common in the river and creek valleys of Edmonton during late winter, and can be heard by anyone who walks in these areas on a warm winter evening. To see this woodland bird is another challenge, however, because this darling of the owls stands only 20 cm tall and is most active at night. When it is seen, the fine white streaks on the head, the dark bill and lack of ear tufts make this bird easy to identify.

GORDON COURT

During winter days, northern saw-whets roost in evergreen trees. At night, they venture out to catch small birds and mammals, and may frequent bird feeders where spilled seed has attracted mice. They often store prey items to be consumed later. In late March, these omens of good luck nest in natural cavities and woodpecker holes, to raise another generation of often overlooked winter residents.

Downy Woodpecker

Picoides pubescens
Michael den Otter

The crunching of boots over freshly fallen snow often obscures the faint tapping of the downy woodpecker as it forages for insects and larvae on the trunks of trees. This small woodpecker (17 cm in length) is a common year-round resident in the Edmonton area and can be found in most city parks and wooded ravines, especially in younger deciduous forest.

The "downy" is an active and unwary bird with a white back and belly, white-spotted black wings and black bars on its white outer tail feathers. Only the males have a red patch on the back of their head. Downies are not very vocal, giving a soft *pik* call year-round, and during courtship, a descending, whinnying laugh.

This woodpecker is a familiar visitor to backyard feeders and is regularly seen enjoying a midwinter snack of suet.

Hairy Woodpecker

Picoides villosus
Michael den Otter

Often confused with its smaller and very similar "downy" cousin, the less common and more reticent hairy woodpecker has a larger bill and lacks black barring on the outer tail feathers. This robin-sized bird (24 cm) produces a sharp *peek*, a much louder call than that of the diminutive downy.

Attracted to suet feeders, hairy woodpeckers are also seen on the upper portions of tree trunks in mature deciduous forest. Using their stiff tail as a brace, they probe and hammer the bark with their chisel-like bill, looking for hidden insects. This soft, erratic tapping is different from the loud drumming heard during the breeding season. By late winter, these woodpeckers rhythmically pound on hollow trees to attract a mate and define their territory.

"Hairies" also use their bill to excavate cavities for nesting. Following a season of use, an abandoned nest site may provide important habitat for another cavity-roosting or nesting species.

WAYNE LYNCH

Pileated Woodpecker

Dryocopus pileatus
Jason O'Donnell

This woodland percussionist is the largest and most famous woodpecker in North America. The cartoon character Woody Woodpecker, with his slicked back, flaming red hair, is based on this bird. The Latin, *Dryocopus*, means "tree cleaver," a good description of what this woodpecker's beak does to decaying trees, stumps and logs as the bird searches for carpenter ants and wood-boring beetle larvae. Pileated woodpeckers stay in Alberta all year, but during the winter, they prefer to roost in old nest cavities in mature deciduous and mixedwood forests.

This crow-sized woodpecker is uncommon, but hard to mistake, with its bright red crest, black body and white flash on the underwing. If you see one, take notice of the feet: two toes forward and two back, a woodpecker adaptation for clinging to the vertical trunks of trees. Walking in the forest, you might only hear this bird's loud, maniacal, laughing call.

Northern Shrike

Lanius excubitor
Christie Dean

The narrow, black mask of the northern shrike hints at the bird's devious and unexpected character. This seemingly passive songbird is actually a fierce predator of other songbirds and small mammals. When it seizes its prey, the shrike makes its kill through a barrage of pecks to the neck, then often impales the victim on a barb or tree branch for later use.

About 25 cm in length, the northern shrike is the smallest predatory bird in the Edmonton region. It is not a common winter visitor to our area, but you may catch sight of one perched in a tree or tall shrub during a winter drive in the country.

EDGAR T. JONES

Besides its characteristic black mask, this bird has a pale gray head and back, black-and-white wings and a black tail with white outer feathers. In flight, the contrasting coloured wings beat feverishly as the bird swoops down on prey or moves from one perch to the next.

Gray Jay

Perisoreus canadensis
Chris Fisher

Just like any really popular kid, the gray jay has a long list of nicknames: whiskey jack, camp robber, moose bird and Canada jay are among the many monikers we use that recognize the notoriety of this northern woods prankster. Gray jays fill cold winter forests with more spirit and mischief than one would expect from such a small package of flesh and feathers.

A bit larger than a robin (29 cm), these jays are year-round residents in much of the forested areas of the province, but in Edmonton, they tend to appear in only our coldest months, as they search far and wide for any edible foods. Often these searches lead them to feeders, particularly in rural areas to the west of the city. Gray jays lay their eggs in the depths of winter in superbly insulated nests, and store foods by coating them with mucous.

Blue Jay

Cyanocitta cristata
Nicole Anderson

Wherever there are feeders and trees for cover, you will find the flamboyant blue jay. Its loud, raucous call, *jay-jay-jay*, is instantly recognizable. This bird will occasionally turn into a mimic, imitating barking dogs, snow blowers and other common neighbourhood sounds.

The boisterous blue jay is easily identified by its vibrant blue back and crest, white belly and straight black bill. About 28 cm long, it sports a black necklace and white patches on its short, rounded wings. Males and females are similar, but try sorting out individuals in your yard by their unique head patterns.

Blue jays are omnivorous, meaning they have a stomach for everything, including fruits, seeds and carrion. However, they have a special affinity for peanuts—shelled or unshelled. Place these delicacies on your backyard feeder shelf and enjoy the show, as one of Edmonton's most aggressive winter songbirds defends and tries to hide its prized possessions.

EDGAR T. JONES

Black-billed Magpie

Pica pica
Melanie Ostopowich

The much-maligned magpie is perhaps the most familiar bird in the Edmonton region; its striking black-and-white markings and long, iridescent tail make it easily recognizable. (Look also for gray-and-white "ghost magpies.") Most often seen alone or in small groups, it usually feeds on the ground and may be seen digging through the snow with its bill. The magpie diet includes a wide range of items, but in your backyard, it will eat almost any scrap you put out, including pet food.

The magpie is large (measuring about 55 cm in length), aggressive and highly intelligent. It is capable of retrieving food under the snow, many months after it was hidden. A very vocal species, its sounds include the common *rak-rak-rak* call and a distinctive, descending *maag*. In past times, magpies were victimized in massive extermination efforts. Fortunately, this practice has generally been abandoned, so this handsome bird can be seen almost anywhere.

Common Raven

Corvus corax
Jason O'Donnell

If ever a bird was suited to ride a noisy Harley-Davidson down the lonely, open highway, it would be a raven. But don't let this shaggy, black beauty fool you. Ravens and their corvid relatives are extremely intelligent; in fact, it would be appropriate to label this species the "Einstein" of birds. Many myths and legends centre around the mystical raven—Blackfoot lore tells of two ravens, one white, one black, who brought the mighty buffalo to the prairies.

WAYNE LYNCH

The raven is one and a half times larger than its sleeker cousin the crow, has a shaggy ruff, and a wedge-shaped tail. The call of the raven is a short, hoarse *kwahk*, easily distinguished from the crow's prolonged, scolding *caw-caw-caw*. The raven is a year-round Alberta resident who prefers boreal and mountain forests, but unlike its migratory cousin, it is increasingly over-wintering in parkland areas like Edmonton.

GORDON COURT

Black-capped Chickadee
Poecile atricapillus
Debbie Galama

With thousands appearing each year on the Edmonton region's Christmas Bird Counts, the black-capped chickadee is one of the most common winter birds in our area. A mere 13 cm, these tiny bundles of energy are able to withstand winter temperatures of -40°C and colder.

A frequent visitor to backyard feeders, this chickadee is easily identified by its black cap and black bib. Particularly fond of sunflower seeds, "black-caps" are also partial to suet and a host of wild foods, including hibernating insects, which they find hidden in the crevices of tree bark. The black-cap's cheery *chick-a-dee-dee-dee* call is one of the most common wild sounds heard in winter.

The Edmonton area's only other chickadee is the closely related boreal (see page 9), which has a brown rather than black cap. The boreal chickadee is seen much less often than the black-capped but will appear where there is suitable conifer habitat. Listen for its nasal *chick-a-day* call.

JOHN ACORN

GORDON COURT

Red-breasted Nuthatch

Sitta canadensis
Debbie Galama

These tiny, year-round residents of the Edmonton region are particularly fond of conifer woods in the river valley and city ravines. Although only 11 cm long, they are quite easy to spot, as they aren't shy and often rocket in and out of backyard feeders. Typically, they forage headfirst down tree trunks and branches, pecking at cracks in the bark for hibernating insects.

Dark-capped and with a slate-blue back, these birds are named for the rusty colour of their breast. However, the black line running through the eye is the best way to distinguish the red-breasted from its larger cousin, the white-breasted nuthatch. The call of the red-breasted, which sounds a little like a tiny toy horn, is a nasal *yank-yank-yank*. A mated pair will also sometimes be heard chattering quietly to each other, particularly in winter, as the birds search for insects or pluck seeds from treetop spruce cones.

White-breasted Nuthatch

Sitta carolinensis
Debbie Galama

Similar in habit and voice to its red-breasted cousin, the white-breasted nuthatch is a regular visitor to well-stocked backyard feeders, favouring those with nuts, sunflower seeds and suet. It likes to grab a hard-shelled nut or seed, wedge it into a crevice in tree bark, then hammer at it until it opens.

EDGAR T. JONES

The 15 cm white-breasted nuthatch sports a dark cap and gray-blue back, but its white, rather than red, breast and clear white face without an eyeline set it apart from its red-breasted kin. Cock an ear to the winter breeze as you stroll along wooded paths, as these birds call commonly throughout the winter months. Their *yarnk-yarnk-yarnk* call is very close to the red-breasted's, but with practice it is possible to tell the two apart.

As you venture further away from city backyards, particularly into stands of mature aspen and poplar, you are more likely to encounter this year-round resident.

European Starling

Sturnus vulgaris
Dave Ealey

Starlings were introduced in North America, about a century ago, by people wanting to establish all of the species contained in the writings of Shakespeare. The species' success has been staggering, there now being an estimated 200 million birds continent-wide. Most of Edmonton's starlings are migratory; however, a few overwinter in our urban areas. Their wide diet allows them to survive on a variety of food items, and they are sometimes attracted to bird feeders.

European starlings look like flying cigars with their dark, stocky bodies, squared-off tails and stubby wings. In winter, adults have blackish plumage covered with conspicuous white speckles, and the normally light bill becomes dark. Starlings seem brash and aggressive, especially when they travel in flocks. Whistles, warbling, harsh chattering, trills and rattles can be heard from both sexes at all times of the year, and their talent for mimicking other birds' songs has confused many a listener.

Bohemian Waxwing

Bombycilla garrulus
Debbie Galama

The elegant Bohemian waxwing descends on our region in large numbers each winter. Drawn by an abundance of mountain ash berries (its favourite winter food), it travels in large, gently twittering flocks that sometimes number in the thousands.

This striking, crested, 20 cm long bird has a delicate cinnamon body, black facial mask and yellow band along the end of its tail. It is named for the small, red, "waxy" spots on the side of its wings, the colour of which is thought to come from the bird's berry diet. The purpose of these spots is unknown.

In any winter flock of Bohemians, you may also find a few cedar waxwings. These smaller (18 cm) cousins usually winter further south, but a few turn up in our region every winter. The best way to tell the two species apart is to note the colour of the undertail coverts—deep rust in the Bohemian, pale yellow in the cedar.

WAYNE LYNCH

Dark-eyed Junco

Junco hyemalis
Chris Fisher

Dark-eyed juncos are among the toughest of Alberta's breeding songbirds, but they still like to avoid the deepest freeze of the Edmonton winter. Juncos are commonly seen foraging in the first and last snows of the winter season, but when the Christmas Bird Count rolls around, junco sightings are hard to come by and sorely missed.

These charcoal sparrows with pink bills and white bellies are frequently seen hopping in short, repetitive bursts by which their delicate feet stir seeds from the ground. Juncos are common and charming visitors to platform feeders, preferring such delicacies as small seeds, cracked grains and finely ground corn. Although quite tame, if alarmed, they give smacking and chipping calls to voice their agitation, and their white outer tail feathers flash as they hastily retreat to the nearest shrub.

Snow Bunting

Plectrophenax nivalis
Alan Hingston

Open fields blanketed with snow and the frigid temperatures of the Alberta winter hardly seem conducive to bird life. Yet, these are the very conditions under which we are most likely to encounter a flock of snow buntings. Known also as "snowbirds" and "snowflakes," these sparrow-sized birds are a combination of brown, black and white, with extensive white wing patches. But it is the flickering black-and-white patterning of the flock in flight that is most distinctive.

EDGAR T JONES

When snow buntings settle to the ground, they seem to disappear against the brown and white of the soil and snow. Here they search for seeds or grain in the stubble. However, the flock, which can number several hundred birds, is soon up and swirling away again in search of other fields. The constant activity of these restless birds is accompanied by a continuous chitter.

WAYNE LYNCH

House Sparrow
Passer domesticus
Dave Ealey

A year-round resident, the house sparrow is a familiar winter bird, at least around human habitations. Somehow, because it is very common, fairly drab and an introduced species to North America, many birders dismiss it. However, we can all learn a lot from this typical songbird, if we are willing to look.

Even in winter, house sparrow sexes are distinct—males have a yellowish bill, black chin, black face mask and gray crown; females feature a pale eyebrow, streaked brownish back and gray underside. This species is stockier than most of our native sparrows and, with its belligerent nature and its flocking behaviour, fares well at bird feeders, often displacing other birds sought after by the feeder watcher.

Four types of *cheep* make up the house sparrow's song, which can be heard throughout the winter. On warm, sunny days in February and March, these birds sing intensively and show conspicuous breeding behaviour.

Pine Siskin
Carduelis pinus
Chris Fisher

CHRIS FISHER

There may be more colourful and melodious birds that appear during Edmonton's winters, but few can surpass the pine siskin for unpredictability. This bird's subtle beauty is often taken for granted during winters when flocks crowd backyard feeders, only to be greatly missed when a snowy season passes without a single pine siskin sighting. Such is the siskin's character: obvious one winter, absent the next.

When they do remain in our neighbourhoods, pine siskins are easily identified as the sparrow-like birds with magical splashes of yellow in their wings and tail. These finches greedily visit niger-filled tube feeders in city and rural backyards, and can often be seen squabbling at feeders in Edmonton's William Hawrelak Park. Siskins generally don't mind being approached as they feed, allowing us intimate appreciation of their gregarious and pugnacious personalities.

Pine grosbeak

WAYNE LYNCH

Evening grosbeak

WAYNE LYNCH

Pine Grosbeak
Pinicola enucleator

Evening Grosbeak
Coccothraustes vespertinus
Marke Ambard

It is always a thrill to have a winter visit from the stunning pine grosbeak. Whether you spot it perched atop a spruce spire, feeding diligently on a snow-covered conifer bow, or at your backyard feeder, this bird will make your heart sing. But listen carefully, because the pine grosbeak might be singing too. With its sweet, warbling song, the pine grosbeak sounds like a winter robin, and many an eager Edmontonian, desperate for spring, has mistaken this bird's voice for our melodious spring songster.

The male pine grosbeak looks like he's been painted a brilliant orange-raspberry red. His gray sides and white wing bars, not to mention the white backdrop of our northern winter, all work to strengthen the vividness of his hues. The colour of females and immatures is a bit less striking; they have a rusty-coloured head and rump, plus gray back and belly.

You also might be lucky enough to see a flock of evening grosbeaks. The male of this species, a striking yellow bird with sharply contrasting black wings and large, conical finch bill, is perhaps the most vividly patterned winter bird of our area. Females and immatures are less conspicuous, with their gray head and back, and light yellow underparts.

Regrettably, these golden gems are becoming increasingly difficult to find within our city limits. Longtime birders will speak nostalgically of times when evening grosbeaks were a regular part of the Edmonton winter scene; however, it's been a long time since those glory days. Fortunately, these birds are regular winter visitors within an easy drive to the north or west of the city. At rural feeders filled with sunflower seeds, evening grosbeaks can still reliably be encountered; they, in turn, make our winters that much more enjoyable.

JOHN ACORN

White-winged Crossbill
Loxia leucoptera
Christie Dean

White-winged crossbills are wonderfully adapted for feeding on conifer seeds. Their telltale crossed bill is used to pry open the scales of cones and their tongue extracts the seeds. During our winters, these crossbills flock to the tops of ornamental and native conifers (mostly spruces). Residents who plant these trees can look forward to the arrival of these birds on cold days, and watching them quietly enjoy a treetop cone feast. White-winged crossbills and their less common relatives, red crossbills, are inconspicuous, and often the only evidence of their activities is a sprinkling of conifer seeds on top of the snow.

Male and female white-winged crossbills are different colours: males are red, whereas females and immatures are a combination of olive-gray and dirty yellow. All have black wings with two distinctive white wing bars. The abundance of these small, sparrow-sized birds (16 cm) fluctuates, increasing or decreasing according to spruce cone productivity.

Common Redpoll
Carduelis flammea
Marke Ambard

Common redpolls are small songbirds (14 cm) able to withstand very severe winter temperatures. Their appearance is unpredictable—they can be abundant one year and rare the next. Favouring niger seed at your backyard feeder, in the wild they rely almost entirely on high energy birch seed. They require a constant energy input in the cold and fill a special pouch in their esophagus

GORDON COURT

with seeds so they can survive the night. Male common redpolls have a heavily streaked rump and sides, a red cap, black chin and reddish breast. The similar females have a light gray breast.

The less common hoary redpoll is much like the common redpoll but is lighter in appearance and has a white rump. There are also birds of intermediate features that sometimes cause confusion. So, rather than fussing over identification, just sit back and enjoy the good-natured company of these birds and marvel at their indomitable northern spirit.

WINTER BIRD SPECIES ~ CONTRIBUTING AUTHORS

MARKE AMBARD
Marke takes advantage of any opportunity for nature exploration, especially if amphibians or birds are involved. Having received his B.Sc. in Conservation Biology from the University of Alberta, he plans to make his living appreciating nature and sharing that appreciation with others. He has spent several summers censusing forest songbirds and is currently employed as a naturalist in the Alberta provincial parks system.

NICOLE ANDERSON
Nicole is a recent graduate of the Environmental and Conservation Sciences (ENCS) program at the University of Alberta. After travelling in Europe she hopes to return to school and pursue a Master's degree. Nicole enjoys spending time in the out-doors—biking, camping, hiking and birding. Her most memorable natural history experience was a recent ENCS birding trip to southern Florida and the Everglades, led by Jim Butler and Chris Fisher.

GORDON COURT
See Chapter 2, page 3.

CHRISTIE DEAN
A native Newfoundlander, Christie came to Alberta to obtain her B.Sc. in Environmental and Conservation Sciences at the University of Alberta. In 1997, she worked for the Edmonton Natural History Club doing amphibian surveys and helping to develop the outline for this book. During this time she enjoyed several experiences with birds, including an owling expedition, bird banding at the Beaverhill Bird Observatory and observing peregrine falcons.

MICHAEL DEN OTTER
Michael's first experiences with wildlife occurred early in life during hiking and fishing trips on Canada's East Coast. His appreciation of the natural world and its diversity deepened with his undergraduate work in conservation biology at the University of Alberta. Michael has worked and volunteered on several different avian research projects and is currently pursuing his interests in human-nature relationships and ecosystem management as a graduate student of rural sociology.

DAVE EALEY
See Chapter 4, page 13.

CHRIS FISHER
See Introduction to Chapter 6, page 21.

DEBBIE GALAMA
See Chapter 7, page 41.

ALAN HINGSTON
Alan came to Alberta from his native England in 1981, and his interest in natural history goes back to his childhood there. Since coming to Alberta, he has been active in all of the Edmonton area natural history clubs; he also started, and for several years edited, the cooperative club newsletter, *Nature Network*. He is a regular participant in the Edmonton and St. Albert Christmas Bird Counts and has organized the Wabamun Lake count for several years.

JASON O'DONNELL
Jason is a Northern Alberta Institute of Technology (NAIT) graduate in both Biological Sciences (1995) and Forestry Technologies (1996), and has worked in a variety of environmental fields including forestry, fisheries and wilderness education. His interest in the environment has led him to design environmental education programs, from which he gained the nature name of "Kinnikinnick." Jason is presently Publicity and Promotions Director of the Edmonton Natural History Club (1998).

MELANIE OSTOPOWICH
Melanie is a fourth year University of Alberta student in the Environmental and Conservation Sciences (ENCS) program (1998). In the summer of 1997, she worked for the Edmonton Natural History Club, along with another student (Christie Dean), to conduct an intensive study of breeding amphibians and also to help develop the outline of content for this publication. Birding has become a favourite pastime, and she is looking forward to extending that hobby into the winter months.

CHRISTINE RICE
Christine Rice is a University of Alberta graduate in conservation biology and at the time of writing was an employee at the Beaverhill Bird Observatory. She has been involved in several local and tropical ornithological field studies and, as a nature enthusiast, is in constant pursuit of new wilderness encounters.

LISA TAKATS
Lisa is eternally enthusiastic and never happier than when she's out in the field admiring wildness. A non-game biologist with the Alberta Conservation Association, she generously volunteers her time and talents to natural history organizations, and to working on raptor and amphibian monitoring projects. A devoted nature enthusiast, Lisa earned her M.Sc. through field studies on barred owl ecology and management, which included pioneering work on call surveying techniques.

CHAPTER SEVEN

THE CHRISTMAS BIRD COUNT PHENOMENON

HISTORY OF THE COUNT
Debbie Galama

The history of the Christmas Bird Count (CBC) began in the late 1800s. This period was a difficult one for North American birds, as unregulated hunting, sport shooting and, in particular, the demand for decorative feathers to adorn women's clothing, caused the loss of hundreds of thousands of birds each year. A large number of species, including egrets, tanagers, orioles, gulls, terns and owls, were victims of the feather trade.

In fact, so popular were feathers, particularly on hats, that *Harper's Bazaar* regularly mentioned them in its fashion column. In the fall of 1884, the stylish woman was advised to wear "dresses bordered with smooth soft feathers and birds' heads"; in the summer of 1899, "whole birds on walking hats" were the rage. Had the practices of unlimited hunting and feather gathering not been stopped, many species would almost certainly be extinct today.

In the late 1800s, hunters began to notice a decline in game bird populations and, not wishing to run out of quarry, began supporting the idea of regulated hunting. These people took no interest, however, in protecting birds they did not hunt, namely songbirds. But, here, fortunately, scientists and naturalists stepped in. In response to the rampant and often inhumane slaughter of birds to support the feather trade, concerned individuals began to establish conservation organizations with the sole purpose of protecting all bird populations for future generations to enjoy.

The American Ornithologists' Union and the Audubon Society were founded during this time, and both sought to raise public awareness of declining bird populations. They accomplished this feat largely through education, explaining the environmental benefits of healthy bird populations (e.g., insect control) and, perhaps most crucially, exposing horrific feather-harvesting practices such as live plucking, in which birds were often left to bleed to death at their nest site. The Audubon Society, in particular, encouraged people to stop wearing bird feathers. The efforts of these groups were successful, culminating in the implementation of various laws in the early 1900s that regulated the hunting and selling of birds.

Emily Murphy 1899

CITY OF EDMONTON ARCHIVES EA-10-1983

The early Audubon Society also produced a magazine entitled *Bird Lore*, which was prepared and edited by a naturalist named Frank M. Chapman. Chapman was a strong supporter of public education as a means of arousing interest in the protection of birds. Thus, in 1900, inspired by a morbid practice known as the side hunt, he organized the very first Christmas Bird Count. The side hunt was a traditional contest between teams or "sides," the winning team

IOM-11   IOM-12   IOM-13   IOM-14

CITY OF EDMONTON ARCHIVES

being the one that shot the most birds on Christmas Day.

Appalled by this meaningless slaughter, Chapman hoped to change people's attitudes by having them count, rather than kill, birds. So, for Christmas Day in 1900, he organized several counts across North America, including two in Canada (one in Toronto; the other in New Brunswick). By any standard, his pioneering efforts were successful, for the Christmas Bird Count is now the largest and oldest bird census in North America. From its meagre beginnings (27 participants in 25 count areas across North America) to its current status (over 40,000 participants in almost 2,000 count areas, 200 of which are in Canada), the count remains one of the highlights of the North American birding year. Standardized regulations, first introduced in 1915, ensure consistency of reporting for all counts.

The first Edmonton area count took place in 1906 with only one participant, Sidney Stansell, a teacher and amateur naturalist. Stansell

Northern goshawk

reported 246 birds of 11 species: northern goshawk, rough-legged hawk, golden eagle, northern hawk owl, Canada (gray) jay, common raven, American crow, hairy woodpecker, pine grosbeak, snow bunting and chickadee (species not mentioned).

Although this first count took place over 90 years ago, it was some time before the city of Edmonton count became firmly established. Between 1906 and 1954 there were only six counts. However, in 1955, renewed interest and vigour led to the beginning of an annual event. Since that year, a count has been held every year (43 consecutive years).

The highlight of Edmonton's involvement in CBCs came in 1986, 80 years after the first count. In that year, local organizers began extensive advertising in the hope of increasing public interest and participation in the count. The impetus for this campaign came partly from *Wildlife '87*, a year of federally sponsored wildlife awareness, celebrating the hundredth anniversary of the establishment of the first Canadian bird sanctuary at Last Mountain Lake, Saskatchewan. The organizers' efforts were more than rewarded as the number of participants jumped from 33 in 1985, to 511 in 1986, and then to an amazing and world record-breaking 1,288 in 1987!

The number of species recorded on Edmonton Christmas Bird Counts has

RAY CROMIE

Great gray owl near Opal

GORDON COURT

also risen, particularly species of owls. The increase in owls is most likely due to the introduction of the "owl prowl," a night-time hunt for these hard-to-find birds. Since the introduction of these prowls, the number of northern saw-whet, great horned, great gray and boreal owls found on counts has risen significantly. To have an idea of how much difference these prowls have made, consider that, prior to 1986, northern saw-whets had been detected on only two previous counts. Since the introduction of the prowls, however, they have been recorded on every count.

Thanks to the participation of many dedicated birders, the city of Edmonton holds many world Christmas Bird Count records, including highest number of participants (1,288 in 1987); highest number of Bohemian waxwings (25,443 in 1986); highest number of merlins (41 in 1986); highest number of pileated woodpeckers (31 in 1995); highest number of black-billed magpies (3,339 in 1994); and highest number of black-capped chickadees (5,096 in 1995).

In addition, Edmonton also holds various Canadian records: highest number of blue jays (1,598 in 1988); highest number of great horned owls (65 in 1988); highest number of northern saw-whet owls (26 in 1993); and highest number of boreal owls (2 in 1988, 1994 and 1995). It is interesting to note that, although there are 108 different species that have been seen on at least one

count, in any one year we have not seen more than 57 different species.

As of the 1997 count—the last before this book was published—annual participation in the Edmonton CBC remained the highest in the world. Each year, birding volunteers count 15,000 to 50,000 birds of 50 or more species. There are currently eight other count areas in the Edmonton region, including Elk Island, Fort Saskatchewan, St. Albert, Coyote Lake, Wabamun Lake, Devon, Tofield and Strathcona (see map on page 47), all part of the more than 70 counts that take place in Alberta every year.

Each year, the results of all "official" North American Christmas Bird Counts are published by the National Audubon Society in its *Field Notes*, which followed *American Birds*, the successor to Chapman's *Bird Lore*. (Some smaller, unofficial counts are not included.) Edmonton region count results may also be published in the *Edmonton Naturalist*, a periodical of the Edmonton Natural History Club, and a provincial compilation appears in the Federation of Alberta Naturalists' *Alberta Naturalist*.

Christmas Bird Counts began as, and continue to be, a pleasurable and productive activity that can be enjoyed by participants of all ages and walks of life who share an interest in viewing and helping our feathered friends. To find out how you can get involved in an Edmonton region CBC, see the last section of this chapter.

DEBBIE GALAMA

Naturalist, teacher, editor and writer, Debbie has been watching birds for over 25 years. A linguist originally from Ontario, she has a special interest in the science of bird song, particularly the similarity between bird communication and human language. Through writing and speaking, Debbie enjoys teaching others, both adults and children, about the wonders of the bird world.

POPULATION TRENDS OF EDMONTON'S OVERWINTERING BIRDS
Geoff Holroyd

Christmas Bird Counts provide us with a very important means of monitoring changes in our winter bird populations. A Christmas Bird Count has been conducted in the city of Edmonton every year since 1955, giving us over 40 continuous years of information. From this count data we can see long-term trends in our overwintering bird populations.

The number of bird species recorded on Christmas Bird Counts in Edmonton has increased from 11 species in 1906, when the count began, to 20 species in 1955, and a peak of 57 species in 1988. This increase is due partly to larger numbers of people participating in the count, and partly to an actual growth in the number and variety of birds in Edmonton. We cannot separate the two effects completely, but we do know that one person did the count in 1906 and a record-breaking 1,288 participated in 1987.

Many species have been attracted by the variety of habitats that an expanding city offers winter birds; for instance, the presence of both ornamental trees and open water have encouraged birds to remain for the winter. The increase in winter bird feeding as a popular hobby has been particularly significant in attracting birds to the Edmonton area. However, many bird species known to the city have declined over the years due to the loss of native habitat and wild places. Other bird populations have remained stable, in spite of changes in habitat and the number of bird feeders in the city. The Edmonton Christmas Bird Count has tracked all these changes, and we will examine them here.

Arrivals due to feeders
The rise in the number of bird feeders is probably the single most important factor that has encouraged birds to overwinter in the Edmonton area.

The house sparrow is a common feeder species that arrived sometime between the 1946 and 1955 Christmas Bird Counts. It has been seen on Christmas Bird Counts every year since 1955 and is now a year-round resident bird. It is much more common in winter and at feeders than another introduced species, the European starling, which tends to migrate south in the fall. According to Christmas Bird Count information, the number of house sparrows in the city peaked in 1969-70, but numbers have been relatively stable since. In 1997, there were 170 house sparrows observed per 10 party-hours. (A party-hour refers to each hour that a group of birders spends in the field during a Christmas Bird Count.)

The red-breasted nuthatch, another regular feeder species, was first reported in 1946, but it is likely this species was present earlier. Initially, it was not common—it was not reported every year, and not more than 5 were reported in a count until 1974, when 15 were counted. Since that time it has been seen on every Edmonton Christmas Bird Count.

The white-breasted nuthatch was first recorded in 1959, then not again until 1969, but has been observed on every Edmonton Christmas Bird Count since. It seems this nuthatch has expanded its range from British Columbia, but the reasons for this expansion are not clear. This species has increased in abundance in the Edmonton area over the past 30 years, but its arrival appears to have had no effect on red-breasted nuthatch numbers.

Pileated woodpeckers were not noted on the Edmonton Christmas Bird Count until 1955 and northern flickers not until 1959. The numbers of both woodpeckers have been variable, and seemed to be in decline until 1980-81, but these species have become more common in the last decade. Although both "pileateds" and flickers use suet feeders, it is not known how important this food source is to their winter survival. Possibly the recent increase in Christmas Bird Count reports of these species is due to the maturing of large trees in the city's river valley.

The numbers of two other, more prevalent woodpeckers, the downy and hairy, have fluctuated in the last 43 years. Both species were most abundant in 1957-1958 and 1973-1975. However, the variation in numbers is much less than for some other species, such as the ruffed grouse and various finches. In other words, in spite of fluctuations, the winter populations of these two woodpeckers are relatively stable. The effect of suet feeders on the survival and population size of these species is not clear.

Pine siskins are welcome visitors to Edmonton bird feeders in winter. Siskins were first recorded on the Edmonton Christmas Bird Count in 1963, then not again until 1971. From 1971 to 1984 their numbers varied greatly, and none at all were seen in six years during that period. Since 1986, they have been counted annually and appear to be increasing in abundance. Almost 1,500 were reported in 1994.

The spectacular evening grosbeak and pine grosbeak were relatively common from 1955 to 1985, although their numbers varied dramatically, with highs of 90 and 50 per 10 party-hours, respectively, down to none seen at all. But both species have been scarce in the Edmonton area since 1986. We do not know why they are less abundant now,

particularly as they use bird feeders in winter, and there are lots of feeders available for them to visit.

The effect of tree planting

Bohemian waxwings became a city winter resident in the mid-1940s, with the planting and maturing of mountain ash as an ornamental tree in the suburbs of Edmonton. By 1956, merlins were staying in the city for the winter, feeding on the waxwings, as well as house sparrows and pigeons. Waxwing numbers in the city oscillated until about 1970, then were low until the mid-1970s. From 1974 to 1983,

Bohemian waxwing on mountain ash

these birds were relatively abundant, but after 1987, sightings again declined. The size of the waxwing population likely fluctuates in relation to food availability in the boreal forest, where this species nests.

The attraction of open water

Open water in the North Saskatchewan River, which has permitted waterfowl to overwinter in the city, is found near the city power and water treatment plants.

Mallards, the most often observed overwintering species, first appeared in winter in Edmonton in 1946. However, they were not common until 1986, when their numbers increased dramatically. In 1990, 4,783 were counted at Christmas; then, just as abruptly, their numbers declined. About 500 mallards have been recorded on the Edmonton Christmas Bird Count in recent years. Mallards that overwinter in Edmonton are typically in poor condition by winter's end.

Although common goldeneye have never been as abundant as mallards, they have been a regular winter residents since 1966. First reported on the count of 1955 (2 were recorded), a maximum of 624 was reported in 1990, the same year that mallard numbers peaked.

A total of 19 species of ducks have been seen on the Edmonton Christmas Bird Count. Species that have been seen only once include wood duck, blue-winged teal, northern shoveler, American wigeon, ring-necked duck, greater scaup, harlequin duck and oldsquaw.

Another unusual waterbird sighted in Edmonton in the Christmas period was a yellow-billed loon, found near the Quesnel Bridge on a small patch of open water in December 1992. After the count, the fire department and divers tried for several days to catch the bird. As temperatures dropped and the area of open water shrank, there was nearly daily media coverage of the plight of the loon and human efforts to catch it. Finally, the loon was captured on Christmas Eve, and a Canadian Wildlife Service employee opted to drive the bird out to the open waters of Wabamun Lake for release, rather than finish his Christmas shopping.

Declines due to habitat loss

The loss of native habitat that has accompanied city expansion has contributed to declines in the numbers of several overwintering bird species.

There are four species of grouse that are resident in the Edmonton area (ruffed and sharp-tailed grouse, gray partridge and ring-necked pheasant). Interestingly, count records show that the numbers of all four species have fluctuated in a regular pattern. These cycles of grouse numbers have peaks approximately 10 years apart and are roughly coincident for all four species. We don't know if these

WAYNE LYNCH

Ring-necked pheasant

peaks are caused by summer nest success, predators, food availability, winter severity or climatic variation.

Sharp-tailed and ruffed grouse numbers have been cyclic since the 1940s, but overall, these two species have become less abundant in the last 50 years. Sharp-tailed grouse numbers have declined from 6 per 10 party-hours on the 1945 Christmas Bird Count to 0.3 in 1990. In some recent years, none have been recorded on the count. The number of ruffed grouse has also decreased—from 3.41 per 10 party-hours in 1959 to 1.02 in 1988. The declines are almost certainly due to the loss of suitable habitat at the edge of the city.

Gray partridge and ring-necked pheasant are both introduced species in North America. They first appeared on the Edmonton Christmas Bird Count in the mid-1940s from releases in or near the city. Their numbers increased until 1961 but have been in decline since. The number of pheasant has decreased dramatically, and this species has not been common on the Edmonton Christmas Bird Count since six were seen in 1966. Numbers of gray partridge have been on a roller-coaster ride since the 1960s. Each successive peak has been lower than the previous peak, and this species is now uncommon in the city of Edmonton. The declines of both species could be due to loss of habitat, reduced releases, or both.

Like these members of the grouse family, the numbers of open country songbirds have declined. Common redpolls were more common before 1981 than any time since. The number of redpolls has decreased from peaks of 40-70 per 10 party-hours before 1981 to less than 10 per 10 party-hours in subsequent years. Snow bunting numbers have been more erratic, but the last high peak was in 1961. In the past 10 years, less than 7 snow buntings per 10 party-miles have been recorded. (A party-mile refers to one mile driven and/or walked by Christmas Bird Count participants.) It appears that these birds of the open field and prairie have lost primary winter habitat to city encroachments.

Population increases due to survey effort

GORDON COURT

Great horned owl

Probably the most substantial increase in species recorded resulting from survey efforts has been in the number of owls. Since 1986, when "owl prowls" were initiated, owl enthusiasts have encouraged birders to listen for owls at night, often using call-playback tapes to stimulate the owls to call. The great horned owl is now the most commonly reported species, followed by the northern saw-whet owl.

Species holding their own

Despite the change in the size of the city, with its resultant change in habitat, and the ongoing popularity of bird feeders, the abundance of some species has not changed at all over the last several years.

Black-billed magpie and blue jay numbers, for instance, have been relatively constant since 1955. Magpies are three times as common as blue jays (900 versus 300 per count, respectively, over the last 20 years). Some folks are not fans of either of these rather bold birds, disliking their habit of eating eggs and nestlings. However, both are native species that fill an ecological niche, and their numbers have not been increasing in the city according to the Christmas Bird Count.

The number of black-capped chickadees has cycled but has not increased over the last 45 years. The pattern of cycling does not appear to be consistent—numbers take a few years to increase, then quickly decrease over 2 years. Declines were noted in 1963-1965, 1975-1977 and 1985-1987. In contrast, the number of boreal chickadees seems to rise and fall on alternate years. This species is far less numerous in Edmonton in winter (20 boreals versus 1,100 black-capped per count).

Results from the Edmonton Christmas Bird Count indicate that the numbers of several overwintering birds in the city of Edmonton have gone through considerable change over the last half century. Although some populations have been stable, others have increased and others have declined dramatically. It is the efforts of hardy and enthusiastic birdwatchers during the count that have made it possible for us to see and study these changes.

GEOFF HOLROYD

Geoff is a research scientist with the Canadian Wildlife Service, an adjunct professor in the Department of Renewable Resources at the University of Alberta, and chairman of the Peregrine Falcon and Burrowing Owl Recovery Teams. He has been president of several non-profit organizations, including the Edmonton Natural History Club and Beaverhill Bird Observatory. Since 1985, he has been actively involved in organizing the Edmonton and Elk Island Christmas Bird Counts.

GETTING INVOLVED IN A COUNT

Chris Fisher

The much-boasted successes of the Edmonton Christmas Bird Count rely not so much on the abundance of bird life as the enthusiasm of participating local area birdwatchers. Unlike many other Christmas Bird Counts across North America, the Edmonton and region counts don't include just serious birders and prominent naturalists. Rather, all people interested in the natural world, no matter what level of experience they might have, are encouraged to participate in this event. By making the process of involvement simple and readily available to anyone interested, these counts satisfy the original purpose of the event: to foster respect and appreciation of nature.

Enthusiastic birders make preparations for the Edmonton Christmas Bird Count, 1988

Christmas bird counts are sponsored by, and the results coordinated and published through, the National Audubon Society in the United States. Count circles (the area where the count takes place), once established, never change, even though habitat conditions and development within the circle can alter the abundance and distribution of bird life within them. The standard count circle has a diameter of 24 km; and for the city of Edmonton count, the centre of the circle is the University of Alberta Farm. All counts sanctioned by the National Audubon Society have count circles of exactly the same size to allow comparison of results between counts and years. The map on the following page shows the nine active count circles of the Edmonton region.

Because of the large area and number of people involved in the city of Edmonton count, it is divided into 15 zones. The count in each zone is coordinated by a zone captain, who assigns key areas to birdwatchers, who search them for birds on count day. The zone captain also collects the results of all zone participants and passes on the tally to the count coordinator, who submits the Edmonton totals to the National Audubon Society.

For someone interested in becoming involved in a count for the first time, the process is very simple. When early December rolls around, you can scan local newspapers and community bulletin boards, or keep a look out for information in mailouts from the Edmonton Natural History Club and Edmonton Bird Club. You can also contact these clubs directly (see Appendix 1); they will have information on all the counts in the Edmonton region. Other places to call include the John Janzen Nature Centre in Edmonton or local bird/nature specialty stores.

During the week prior to count day, a public presentation known as the *Birds of Christmas* is featured at the Provincial Museum of Alberta (see Appendix 1 for the museum address and phone number). It is at this event that all the information needed to participate in the the city of Edmonton count is made available. Zone captains can sign up eager participants, following an animated presentation on the identification of birds expected on count day. The *Birds of Christmas* is an enjoyable social event for many, and a natural preamble to count day.

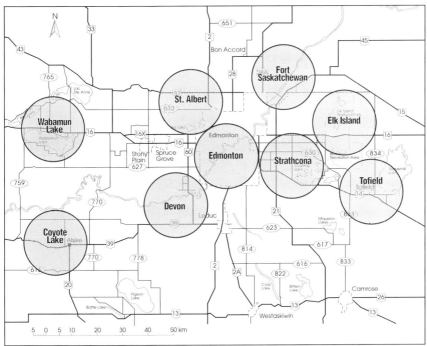

Edmonton region count circles for Christmas Bird Count

For those who want to participate in a Christmas Bird Count, probably the biggest decision to make is the kind of involvement they want to have. Opportunities exist for all levels of skill, interest and mobility. Generally, participants in Edmonton region counts fall into one of three categories: feeder watchers, bush beaters and owl prowlers.

Feeder watching

For those just learning about winter birds, or those who want to stay inside, feeder watching can be an extremely rewarding experience. This type of participation does not require the time commitment of other count activities and frequently turns in some of the best results of the day. Feeder watchers need only keep an eye on the bird activity in their backyards on count day, as they go about their regular routine. Literally hundreds of people participate in this way on Edmonton area counts.

As there is often only a limited number of species that frequent yards at this time of year, the identification of species is relatively easy. Counting the number of individual birds that appear is another matter, however. As birds tend to come and go, their numbers can vary considerably, and there is a very real risk of duplicate counting of individuals. Counting peak numbers for a species present at any one time is probably the most accurate way of estimating the maximum number of different individuals of each species.

Bush beating

Bush beaters strike out during the early daylight hours to walk the trails, crisscross woodlots and ravines, and search from country roads. Armed with binoculars, these stalwart participants search out the familiar calls that echo in the winter woods, and scan open fields for a brief flash of flight. Many bush beaters begin count day before dawn, discussing final strategies with zone captains, before taking to the trail. Others join in partway through the day to investigate an assigned area. Field techniques such as "pishing" (see Chapter 4 for a description) are very useful for bush beaters because birds are readily drawn to these sounds during the winter.

Bush beating is popular as it encourages people to experience winter bird life first hand, at a time of year when many people do not think of spending prolonged periods outdoors.

Birdwatchers on pre-Christmas Bird Count field trip, Whitemud Ravine, Edmonton

HARRY STELFOX

The owl prowl

Many people who are really keen on the Christmas Bird Count experience join an owl prowl. Because there are several species of night-calling owls around during the winter months, owl prowlers get going early. By 12:01 a.m. on count day, Edmonton area count circles are alive with the taped vocalizations of selected owl species. With any luck, these specially designed recordings will elicit a call from a genuine bird.

Before the bush beaters have even begun their treks, some owl prowlers have already put in six or seven hours and are eager to share their morning's findings. The efforts of the owl prowlers are a great motivation for other count participants, and their findings have done much to unravel the mysteries of owl abundance and distribution in the Edmonton area in winter.

Edmonton and region Christmas Bird Counts offer challenges and rewards as diverse as the people who take part in the counts. Many people choose to become involved because it gives them an excuse to study the birds that have

been venturing into their backyard. For these people, seeing the subtle differences between black-capped and boreal chickadees is an experience as important as that of the "hard lister" who finds that one rarity while searching diligently over masses of common wintering ducks.

Many people choose to get involved in the Christmas Bird Count because of the social interaction. Birdwatchers are a friendly sort, and meetings down a wintry trail rarely end without everyone in smiles. Christmas Bird Counts enable people interested in nature to come together at least once a year and share their common interest. To facilitate this interaction, the city of Edmonton count day ends with a potluck supper and wrap-up Count Call that summarizes the results and rare finds. Laughs and good-natured boasting are as much a part of this evening as the results obtained from the daylong search.

Christmas Bird Counts also promote environmental awareness. By becoming increasingly aware of our natural surroundings, we become more understanding and appreciative of birds, other wildlife and their habitat needs. When people appreciate the natural world, natural areas and wildlife are given a higher priority in their lives, ultimately contributing to an increased conservation ethic in our society. These are the subtle effects of the Christmas Bird Count experience, which evolve with each species observed and with each laugh shared with a kindred spirit.

A HELP LIST FOR INFORMATION ON EDMONTON'S WINTER BIRDS

AGENCIES AND ORGANIZATIONS

The following agencies and organizations can give you information on winter birds in the Edmonton region.

Edmonton Bird Club
Box 1111
Edmonton, AB T5J 2M1

Edmonton Natural History Club
Box 1582
Edmonton, AB T5J 2N9

Federation of Alberta Naturalists
Box 1472
Edmonton, AB T5J 2N5
Ph. (403) 427-8124

**Natural Resources Service
(Fish and Wildlife)
Alberta Environmental Protection
Edmonton Metropolitan Office**
4515 - 122 Ave.
Edmonton, AB T5L 2W4
Ph. (403) 427-3574.

Provincial Museum of Alberta
12845 - 102 Ave.
Edmonton, AB T5N 0M6
Ph. (403) 453-9100.

BIRD HOTLINE

Sponsored by the Wild Bird General Store, Edmonton Bird Club and Edmonton Natural History Club. Call this number to find out about interesting and unusual bird sightings, and detailed information on how to find the bird(s). Covers northern Alberta, but most sightings are in the Edmonton region.

Phone: (403) 433-2473

NATURE CENTRES AND PARKS

Visit any of these places to see and/or get information on winter birds in the Edmonton region.

**Beaverhill Nature Centre
Town of Tofield**
Box 30
Tofield, AB T0B 4J0
Ph. (403) 662-3191

Elk Island National Park
Site 4, RR #1
Fort Saskatchewan, AB T8L 2N7
Ph. (403) 922-5790 or 992-2950

**John Janzen Nature Centre
City of Edmonton**
P.O. Box 2359,
Edmonton, AB T5J 2R7
Ph. (403) 496-2939

**River Valley Outdoor Centre
City of Edmonton**
10125 - 97 Ave.
Edmonton, AB T5K 0B3
Ph. (403) 496-7275

**Strathcona Wilderness Centre
c/o Recreation, Parks and
Culture Department
County of Strathcona**
2025 Oak St.
Sherwood Park, AB T8A 0W9
(403) 922-3939

PLEASE NOTE:

At the end of January, 1999, the area code for the Edmonton region will change from (403) to (780).

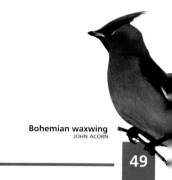

Bohemian waxwing
JOHN ACORN

SPECIES LISTS FROM EDMONTON AREA CHRISTMAS BIRD COUNTS

Dave Ealey

The following lists were compiled from the results for Christmas Bird Counts held in the Edmonton region from 1987 to 1996, inclusive. The following locations were included: Edmonton, Fort Saskatchewan, St. Albert, Strathcona, Tofield and Wabamun Lake. Although counts were not held in each location every year, the results seem to be a reasonable snapshot of relative frequency of species sightings.

The different lists are based on the following criteria:

- each species seen in one location in one year constituted a single "sighting"—the maximum number of sightings in this analysis, based on the total number of counts that took place, was 56

- no location carried any greater weight than any other location (so city of Edmonton sightings did not outrank those from regional sites)

- if the number of sightings for a species was 75 percent or more (42 - 56) of the potential sightings, then it was considered an **"A" list** bird (common or expected most years)

- sightings of more than 25 percent and less than 75 percent (15 to 41 sightings) resulted in the species being placed on the **"B" list** (fairly common or of fairly regular occurrence)

- sightings of 25 percent or less (1 - 14 sightings) meant that the bird species was placed on the **"C" list** (uncommon to rare).

We suggest that you use these lists to keep track of the winter birds you see; whenever you find a species new to you, just make a check mark beside the bird's name. If you observe a species not yet on a list just add it to the end of the "C" list.

"A" LIST SPECIES
(Common or Expected Most Years)

- ❍ ruffed grouse
- ❍ rock dove
- ❍ great horned owl
- ❍ downy woodpecker
- ❍ hairy woodpecker
- ❍ pileated woodpecker
- ❍ northern shrike
- ❍ blue jay
- ❍ black-billed magpie
- ❍ common raven
- ❍ black-capped chickadee
- ❍ boreal chickadee
- ❍ white-breasted nuthatch
- ❍ snow bunting
- ❍ pine grosbeak
- ❍ common redpoll
- ❍ evening grosbeak
- ❍ house sparrow

"B" LIST SPECIES
(Fairly Common or of Fairly Regular Occurrence)

- ❍ mallard
- ❍ common goldeneye
- ❍ bald eagle
- ❍ northern goshawk
- ❍ merlin
- ❍ gray partridge
- ❍ ring-necked pheasant
- ❍ sharp-tailed grouse
- ❍ snowy owl
- ❍ northern saw-whet owl
- ❍ three-toed woodpecker
- ❍ black-backed woodpecker
- ❍ northern flicker
- ❍ gray jay
- ❍ American crow
- ❍ red-breasted nuthatch
- ❍ brown creeper
- ❍ golden-crowned kinglet
- ❍ European starling
- ❍ Bohemian waxwing
- ❍ dark-eyed junco
- ❍ white-winged crossbill
- ❍ hoary redpoll
- ❍ pine siskin

Common raven
WAYNE LYNCH

"C" LIST SPECIES
(Uncommon to Rare)

- ⊖ yellow-billed loon
- ⊖ pied-billed grebe
- ⊖ horned grebe
- ⊖ red-necked grebe
- ⊖ western grebe
- ⊖ double-crested cormorant
- ⊖ great blue heron
- ⊖ snow goose
- ⊖ Canada goose
- ⊖ trumpeter swan
- ⊖ gadwall
- ⊖ American wigeon
- ⊖ American black duck
- ⊖ blue-winged teal
- ⊖ northern shoveler
- ⊖ northern pintail
- ⊖ green-winged teal
- ⊖ canvasback
- ⊖ redhead
- ⊖ ring-necked duck
- ⊖ lesser scaup
- ⊖ harlequin duck
- ⊖ oldsquaw
- ⊖ bufflehead
- ⊖ Barrow's goldeneye
- ⊖ hooded merganser
- ⊖ red-breasted merganser
- ⊖ common merganser
- ⊖ ruddy duck
- ⊖ northern harrier
- ⊖ sharp-shinned hawk
- ⊖ Cooper's hawk
- ⊖ red-tailed hawk
- ⊖ rough-legged hawk

- ⊖ golden eagle
- ⊖ gyrfalcon
- ⊖ American coot
- ⊖ killdeer
- ⊖ ring-billed gull
- ⊖ California gull
- ⊖ glaucous gull
- ⊖ northern hawk owl
- ⊖ barred owl
- ⊖ great gray owl
- ⊖ long-eared owl
- ⊖ short-eared owl
- ⊖ boreal owl
- ⊖ belted kingfisher
- ⊖ loggerhead shrike
- ⊖ Steller's jay
- ⊖ horned lark
- ⊖ mountain chickadee
- ⊖ winter wren
- ⊖ Townsend's solitaire
- ⊖ American robin
- ⊖ varied thrush
- ⊖ brown thrasher
- ⊖ cedar waxwing

- ⊖ yellow-rumped warbler
- ⊖ American tree sparrow
- ⊖ song sparrow
- ⊖ Lincoln's sparrow
- ⊖ white-throated sparrow
- ⊖ Harris's sparrow
- ⊖ white-crowned sparrow
- ⊖ northern cardinal
- ⊖ yellow-headed blackbird
- ⊖ rusty blackbird
- ⊖ Brewer's blackbird
- ⊖ common grackle
- ⊖ purple finch
- ⊖ house finch
- ⊖ red crossbill
- ⊖ *other* _____
- ⊖ *other* _____
- ⊖ *other* _____
- ⊖ *other* _____
- ⊖ *other* _____

Gyrfalcon

RAY CROMIE

GENERAL INFORMATION ON BIRDS

Bovey, Robin. 1990, rev. ed. Birds of Edmonton. Lone Pine Publishing, Edmonton, Alberta.
Provides information on 75 birds found in and around Edmonton; each description comes with habitat symbols and a colour illustration. At back of book is a chapter on how to attract birds with feeders, nest boxes and backyard landscaping; small section on bird photography.

Dekker, Dick. 1998, rev. ed. Prairie waters: wildlife at Beaverhills Lake, Alberta. The University of Alberta Press, Edmonton, Alberta.
A friendly, informative book on the ecology and wildlife of Beaverhill Lake, near Tofield, Alberta. Many chapters on birds, including one on the famous geese migrations. Illustrated with fine colour photographs.

Godfrey, W. Earl. 1986, rev. ed. The birds of Canada. National Museum of Canada, Ottawa, Ontario.
A Canadian "bird bible," this coffee table-sized book has details on all the birds known to Canada and its coastal waters. Includes Canadian range maps and colour illustrations (latter separate from rest of text).

Semenchuk, Glen P., ed. 1992. The atlas of breeding birds of Alberta. Federation of Alberta Naturalists, Edmonton, Alberta.
Coffee table-sized book with a page of life history information for each bird species; includes high quality colour photographs and Alberta range maps based on five years of "atlassing." Also has brief description and colour photo for several common Alberta migrants.

FIELD GUIDES

Chapman, Ross. 1991. The discoverer's guide to Elk Island National Park. Lone Pine Publishing and The Friends of Elk Island Society, Edmonton, Alberta.
Colourfully illustrated with brief descriptions of the park's birds, plants and animals. Has sections on habitat and geology plus a useful park trail guide.

Fisher, Chris, and John Acorn. 1998. Birds of Alberta. Lone Pine Publishing, Edmonton, Alberta.
An up-to-date, soft-cover guide to over 300 bird species found in Alberta; includes the information necessary for field identification, Alberta range maps, colour illustrations and text that brings out the uniqueness and character of each bird species. Also has a map and descriptions of Alberta's top birding sites.

McGillivray, W. Bruce, and Glen Semenchuk. 1998. A field guide to Alberta birds. Federation of Alberta Naturalists, Edmonton, Alberta.
A new field guide to Alberta's breeding birds and migrants. Has colour photos, inset photos of eggs, and up-to-date Alberta range maps. Text includes a detailed "field checklist" for identification and a colour bar showing what months each species can be seen in Alberta.

Peterson, Roger Tory. 1990, 3d ed. A field guide to western birds. Houghton Mifflin Co., Boston and New York.
A well-known field guide used by many birders; emphasis is on identifying species in the field. A page of colour illustrations accompanies a page of text. Range maps at back of book.

Robbins, Chandler S., Bertel Bruun and Herbert S. Zim. 1983. A guide to field identification. Birds of North America. Golden Press, New York.
A pocket-sized book with short descriptive text, North American range maps and small colour illustrations for each species. Information is a little dated, but the book is still very good for beginners.

Saley, Henry, Harry Stelfox and Dave Ealey. 1995. Nature walks & Sunday drives 'round Edmonton. Edmonton Natural History Club, Edmonton, Alberta.
Explore 25 of the best watchable wildlife sites in the Edmonton region with this guide. Special features for each site include what birds you are likely to see. Maps show how to access each site.

Scott, S.L. 1987. A field guide to the birds of North America. National Geographic Society, Washington, D.C.
A helpful field guide. Shows North American range for each species, and each page of write-ups has an accompanying page of colour illustrations.

ATTRACTING BIRDS AND BACKYARD FEEDING

Butler, Elaine. 1991. Attracting birds. Lone Pine Publishing, Edmonton, Alberta.
A primer on how to bring the birds in. Describes the basics of feeder types and feeder mixes, and how to provide water; also has sections on bird houses, providing nesting material, when to put out food, how to landscape your yard and trouble-shooting.

Pearman, Myrna. 1989. Winter bird feeding. An Alberta guide. Ellis Bird Farm, Lacombe, Alberta.
A comprehensive, attractively illustrated guide to attracting winter birds. Has lots of information on bird feeders and feeder mixes, plus suet, gourmet treats and water; also a chapter on Alberta's feeder birds with fine black-and-white drawings. Includes a chapter on problem-solving and a resource file.

Self, Charles R. 1985. Making birdhouses & feeders. Sterling Publishing Co., Inc., New York.
Everything you ever wanted to know about building feeders and bird houses. Has chapters on choosing wood, construction materials, tools, joints, finishes, designs and bird foods.

Waldon, Bob. 1990. A prairie guide to feeding winter birds. Western Producer Prairie Books, Saskatoon, Saskatchewan.
Lots of bird lore and lots of humour. Has sections on bird feeding and feeders, and how to deal with backyard birding problems, plus a chapter on several overwintering prairie birds. Illustrations are black-and-white. Appendix has gourmet recipes, and illustrations to help you build the feeder of your dreams.

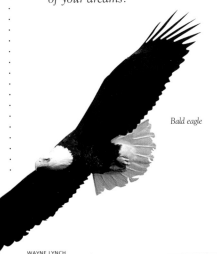

Bald eagle

WAYNE LYNCH